Essentially Feminine Knits

Editor

Erica Smith

Translation

Carol Huebscher Rhoades

Technical Editor and Illustrator

Therese Chynoweth

Art Director

Liz Quan

Cover & Interior Design

Lora Lamm

Production

Katherine Jackson

*Many thanks to Anne, Astrid, Bodil, Else, Inge,
Norma, and Susanne who helped with the knitting.*

 Interweave Press LLC
201 East Fourth Street
Loveland, CO 80537
interweave.com

Printed in China by RR Donnelley Shenzhen

Library of Congress Cataloging-in-Publication Data

Samsøe, Lene Holme.
  [Mere feminin strik. English]
  Essentially feminine knits : 25 must-have chic designs /
Lene Holme Samsøe.
      p. cm.
  Includes bibliographical references and index.
  ISBN 978-1-59668-784-4 (pbk.)
  1. Knitting--Patterns. I. Title.
  TT820.S23513 2012
  746.43'2041--dc23
                          2011051288

10 9 8 7 6 5 4 3 2

Essentially Feminine Knits

Knits

25 Must-Have Chic Designs

Lene Holme Samsøe

INTERWEAVE.
Interweave.com

Contents

Foreword   *5*

*How to Use this
  Book*   *6*

Garter Stitch
  Patterns

Rita   12
Fiona   16
Siri   22
Tara   26
Rosita   30

Leaf Patterns

Palma   38
Lily   44
Hella   50
Nikita   54
Bella   60

Structure Patterns

Gerda   66
Raya   72
Smilla   78
Paula   84
Penelope   88

Cable Patterns

Viola   96
Lea & Lola   100
Petra   108
Wilma   112
Amanda   118

Lace Patterns

Lana   126
Cecilia   132
Coco   136
Vicky   142
Holly   146

Yarns   *149*

*Sources for
  Yarns*   *150*

Index   *151*

Foreword

All you knit is love!

If you are crazy about knitting, you already know that creating a knitted garment is the perfect antidote to the busy lives we lead.

Knitting can be a social hobby, which you can do with like-minded people at a café, as well as a solitary respite from a busy workday, in which you enjoy knitting's meditative effects and let your thoughts flow out in all directions.

In this book you'll find projects for any occasion. There are a couple of small, quick projects that you can almost make while watching the TV news, some garter-stitch sweaters you can work on while having a rewarding conversation, and complicated-patterned tops that stretch your mind just as much as Sudoku. Each in its own way can be the perfect knit garment.

Knitting is also perfect as a present—love is knitted into each and every stitch!

The twenty-five designs in this book range widely from delightful and decorative lace patterns to simple and casual sweaters in nothing but garter stitch. So, grab your needles and beautiful yarns.

Lene Holme Samsøe

How to Use This Book

Sizes

Most of the garments in the book are given in four sizes, usually Small, Medium, Large, and Extra-large. The measurement chart below shows what parts of the body to measure for the individual sizes.

When choosing sizes, it is a good idea to compare the measurements on the model you want to knit with your own measurements. Also compare the pattern measurements with those of a sweater you like wearing so you can get a sense of how it will fit. All the garments shown in this book are, with few exceptions, knitted up in size Small and shown on models who are size 36.

Each pattern lists the measurements of the finished garment. The chest is the sweater's circumference just under the underarm. Don't forget that knitting is elastic, so the chest of the sweater should not be much larger than your actual chest size.

Also note that sleeves, as a rule, are longer on smaller sizes than on larger sizes. It's not a mistake but is designed that way because the back is wider on large sizes than on small sizes and, correspondingly, the sleeve cap is longer on the large sizes than on the small ones.

Adjustments

If your measurements differ quite a bit from those given in the measurement chart below, you can still change the pattern, in much the same way as you would adjust the cutting lines on a sewing pattern.

The models are calculated for a body length of about 64½–67¾" (164–172 cm). If you are taller or shorter, it might be necessary, for example, to knit the sleeves longer or shorter than given. The same applies if you have longer or shorter arms than average for your height. If you are much taller or shorter than average, you might also need to knit the garment with longer or shorter side seams. If the model has a defined waist, make sure that the waist hits at the right height.

SIZES		S 34–36	M 38–40	L 42	XL 44–46
CHEST	in	32¼	35	37¾	40¼
	cm	82	89	96	102
WAIST	in	25½	27½	30	32¼
	cm	65	70	76	82
HIP	in	36¼	38½	40¼	42½
	cm	92	98	102	108

Materials

I almost exclusively use yarns in natural materials such as wool and silk. At the back of the book you can find descriptions of all the yarns. If you want to substitute yarns, try to match the original yarn's yards/ounces (or meters/grams) and the recommended gauge. It is a good idea to buy extra yarn if you are not using the one suggested in the pattern.

Instructions

Always read the pattern all the way through before you start knitting. A number of pattern elements apply generally to every pattern in the book and are not explained in every single pattern. The following sections contain the information that applies to all the patterns in the book.

Gauge

The gauge tells you how many stitches there should be in a 4" (10 cm) width and sometimes (when necessary) how many rows in length of 4" (10 cm).

Before you begin knitting a pattern, you must be certain that you are working at the same gauge as given in the pattern. To do that, you must knit a gauge swatch! Knit with the same needles and in the same pattern as the gauge specifies, for example, stockinette. The swatch should be somewhat larger than 4 x 4" (10 x 10 cm) so, for example, cast on 30 stitches and work until the swatch is about 5½" (14 cm) long and then bind off.

Lay the swatch flat on the table and place pins at each side to mark off 4" (10 cm) in width. If you also want to check the number of rows in length, do that the same way. Now count how many stitches there are between the pins across and, if desired, how many rows are between the pins in length. If you have enclosed exactly the same number of stitches and/or rows as the gauge given in the pattern, you can merrily go on your way!

If your piece has more stitches across than specified in the pattern, then you've knitted too tightly and should try one U.S. (½ metric) size larger needles. Vice versa, if you have fewer stitches across than specified in the pattern, you have knitted too loosely and must try again with one U.S. (½ metric) size smaller needles. If your gauge varies quite a lot from the pattern's, try needles two U.S. (1 full metric)

size larger or smaller. If your gauge differs only a little bit from the pattern's, you might try knitting the WS rows with a U.S. (½ metric) size smaller needle or knit the RS rows with a U.S. (½ metric) size larger needle. This advice pertains primarily to stockinette knit pieces because many people work knit rows a little tighter than purl rows.

As a rule, it is very important that you maintain the gauge across the width and the number of stitches. For that reason, in this book, I've almost never listed the gauge for length—the number of rows in 4" (10 cm).

It pays to take some time with the gauge swatch, because even small variations in the gauge can make a big difference in the size of the finished garment. If you have 19 sts in 4" (10 cm) instead of 20 as specified in the pattern, it actually means that the sweater will be almost a full size larger than you might expect!

Edge Stitches

In most of the patterns in the book, the outermost stitch at each side is an edge stitch. When garment pieces are sewn together, the stitching goes inside the edge stitches. Always knit the edge stitches on every row and do not include them in the pattern. Edge stitches are not shown on the charts. All increases and decreases (for example, along the side seams) are worked inside the edge stitches so you can seam or pick up and knit stitches (or the front bands, for example) inside the edge stitches, without disturbing the decreases and increases.

Set Stitches Aside

When the instructions say to "set stitches aside" or "place on a holder," it means that you should neither work nor bind off those stitches. You set stitches aside by placing them on a stitch holder, a strong length of yarn, a knitting needle, or a safety pin.

Charts

Many knitting patterns are more clearly explained with the help of charts rather than more words. In the charts, I have chosen the same symbols throughout the book and many of the symbols resemble the steps they describe. Overviews and explanations for all the symbols are listed on page 9.

Finishing

Careful finishing can sometimes make a garment that wasn't very smoothly knitted look wonderful, but, unfortunately, the opposite applies as well—sloppy finishing can ruin the nicest piece of knitting.

When you sew the seams, it is important that the seam stitches align precisely in the same line of knit stitches all the way up, as, for example, along the side seam. If you seam from the RS with a mattress stitch, it is very important to make sure you are sewing directly inside the edge stitch and not into the space between the edge stitch and the adjacent stitch. To make seaming smoother, you can split the yarn and seam with one ply, using a blunt tapestry needle.

All the models in the book are wet-blocked, spun (centrifuged) with the lowest number of revolutions (400), laid out to the correct measurements on a hand towel over a floor heater, and left flat until completely dry. Turn the pieces once so that the same side is not facing down the whole time. Of course, you can dry the garment in other ways but always dry flat, not hanging.

Abbreviations

beg	begin, beginning
BO	bind off
cm	centimeter(s)
cn	cable needle
CO	cast on
dbl dec	dec to eliminate 2 stitches at the same time = sl 1, k2tog, psso
dec	decrease
dpn	double-pointed needles
g	gram(s)
in	inch(es)
inc	increase
k	knit
k1f&b	knit into front and then back of stitch = 2 sts
k2tog	knit 2 together
k3tog	knit 3 together
M1	Make 1 increase
m	meter(s)
mm	millimeter(s)
p	purl
p2tog	purl 2 together
pm	place marker
psso	pass slipped stitch over
rem	remain(s), remaining
rep	repeat
rnd(s)	round(s)
RS	right side
s2kp	slip 2, knit 1, psso
sl	slip
slm	slip marker
ssk	slip 2 stitches knitwise, one at a time, from left needle to right needle, insert left needle tip through both front loops and knit together from this position (1 stitch decreased)
st(s)	stitch(es)
St st	stockinette stitch = knit on RS and purl on WS
tbl	through back loop
WS	wrong side
Wyif	with yarn in front
Wyib	with yarn in back
yd	yard(s)
yo	yarnover
*	repeat starting point
( )	alternate measurements and/or instructions

Symbol Key

▢	k on RS; p on WS
•	p on RS; k on W
ℓ	k1 tbl on RS; p1 tbl on WS
o	yo
╱	k2tog
╲	ssk
↗	p2tog
↘	ssp
↗	k3tog
↗	sl 1, k2tog, psso
ʌ	sl 2 as if to k2tog, k1, p2sso
↖	k3tog tbl
M	M1
V	sl 1 wyb on RS; sl 1 wyf on WS
₴	kf&b in strand between sts
●	bobble (see Stitch Guide)
▨	no stitch

sl 1 st onto cn, hold in back, k1, k1 from cn

sl 1 st onto cn, hold in front, k1, k1 from cn

sl 1 st onto cn, hold in back, k1, p1 from cn

sl 1 st onto cn, hold in front, p1, k1 from cn

sl 1 st onto cn, hold in back, k2, k1 from cn

sl 2 sts onto cn, hold in front, k1, k2 from cn

sl 1 st onto cn, hold in back, k2, p1 from cn

sl 2 sts onto cn, hold in front, p1, k2 from cn

sl 2 sts onto cn, hold in back, k1, p2 from cn

sl 1 st onto cn, hold in front, p2, k1 from cn

sl 2 sts onto cn, hold in back, k2, k2 from cn

sl 2 sts onto cn, hold in front, k2, k2 from cn

sl 1 st onto cn, hold in back, k3, p1 from cn

sl 3 sts onto cn, hold in front, p1, k3 from cn

sl 2 sts onto cn, hold in back, k3, p2 from cn

sl 3 sts onto cn, hold in front, p2, k3 from cn

sl 2 sts onto cn, hold in front, sl 1 st to second cn, hold in back, k2, p1 from back cn, k2 from front cn

sl 3 sts onto cn, hold in back, k3, k3 from cn

sl 3 sts onto cn, hold in front, k3, k3 from cn

sl 1 st onto cn, hold in back, k3, (k1, k1 tbl, k1) from cn

sl 3 sts onto cn, hold in front, (k1, k1 tbl, k1) in next st, k3 from cn

sl 4 sts onto cn, hold in back, k4, k4 from cn

sl 4 sts onto cn, hold in front, k4, k4 from cn

sl 2 sts onto cn, hold in back, k4, (k1f&b) twice from cn

sl 4 sts onto cn, hold in front, (k1f&b) twice, k4 from cn

sl 1 st onto cn, hold in back, sl 6 sts to second cn, hold in back, k1, (p1, k4, p1) from second cn, k1 from first cn

sl 3 sts onto cn, hold in back, k5, [(k1f&b) twice, k1] from cn

sl 5 sts onto cn, hold in front, (k1f&b) twice, k1, then k5 from cn

sl 4 sts onto cn, hold in back, k6, [(k1f&b) twice, k2] from cn

sl 6 sts onto cn, hold in front, (k1f&b) twice, k2, then k6 from cn

sl 6 sts onto cn, hold in back, k6, k6 from cn

sl 6 sts onto cn, hold in front, k6, k6 from cn

Garter Stitch Patterns

Garter stitch is one of the easiest patterns to knit. You knit all the stitches on every row for an even, ridged structure that looks great on both sides. On some of the garments in this section, garter stitch is used to great effect when garter ridges and smooth stockinette stripes alternate on right and wrong sides.

Rita
Garter Stitch Sweater with Raglan Shaping

This totally simple and eminently practical garter stitch raglan sweater has overlapping fronts. It's a good project for those who don't have much knitting experience. The yarn is a rustic tweed, but the sweater would also look great in another yarn, perhaps the same combination used in Fiona, shown on page 16.

		S	M	L	XL
BUST	in	35½	39	42	45½
	cm	90	99	106.5	115.5
TOTAL LENGTH	in	21¾	22	22¾	23¾
	cm	55	56	58	60.5

Yarn Aran weight (Medium #4). Shown in: Rowan Felted Tweed Aran (50% merino wool, 25% alpaca, 25% viscose; 95 yd [87 m]/50 g); cork #721, 10 (11, 11, 12) balls.

Needles U.S. size 9 (5.5 mm): straight and 32" (80 cm) circular (cir). Adjust needle sizes if necessary to obtain the correct gauge. U.S. size 7 (4.5 mm): straight or 24" (60 cm) circular for collar.

Notions Stitch markers (m), tapestry needle, 2 large snaps, 1–1¼" (25–30 mm).

Gauge 15 sts and 29 rows = 4" (10 cm) in garter st on larger needles.

Back

With larger needles, CO 75 (81, 87, 93) sts.

Work in k1, p1 rib for 3 rows. Cont in garter st (knit every row) until piece measures 3¼" (8 cm), ending with a WS row.

NEXT ROW (DEC): K1, k2tog, knit to last 3 sts, ssk, k1—2 sts dec'd. Cont dec every 3¼" (8 cm) three more times—67 (73, 79, 85) sts rem.

Work even until piece measures 12½" (32 cm), ending with a WS row.

BO 5 (6, 7, 8) sts at beg of next 2 rows—57 (61, 65, 69) sts. Place rem sts on a holder.

Left Front

With larger needles, CO 47 (50, 53, 56) sts.

Work in k1, p1 rib for 3 rows. Cont in garter st until piece measures 3¼" (8 cm), ending with a WS row.

NEXT ROW (DEC): K1, k2tog, knit to end—1 st dec'd. Cont dec every 3¼" (8 cm) three more times—43 (46, 49, 52) sts rem.

Work even until piece measures 12½" (32 cm), ending with a WS row.

BO 5 (6, 7, 8) sts at side at beg of next row—38 (40, 42, 44) sts. Place rem sts on a holder.

Right Front

With larger needles, CO 47 (50, 53, 56) sts.

Work in k1, p1 rib for 3 rows. Cont in garter st until piece measures 3¼" (8 cm), ending with a WS row.

NEXT ROW (DEC): Knit to last 3 sts, ssk, k1—1 st dec'd. Cont dec every 3¼"

(8 cm) three more times—43 (46, 49, 52) sts rem.

Work even until piece measures 12½" (32 cm), ending with a RS row.

BO 5 (6, 7, 8) sts at side at beg of next row—38 (40, 42, 44) sts. Place rem sts on a holder.

Sleeves

With larger needles, CO 32 (34, 36, 38) sts.

Work in k1, p1 rib for 3 rows. Cont in garter st until piece measures 3 (2½, 2½, 2)" (7.5 [6.5, 6.5, 5] cm), ending with a WS row.

NEXT ROW (INC): K1, M1 knit to last st, M1, k1—2 sts inc'd.

Cont increase row every 3 (2½, 2½, 2)" (7.5 [6.5, 6.5, 5) cm) 4 (5, 5, 6) more times—42 (46, 48, 52) sts.

Work even until piece measures 17 (17, 16½, 16¼)" (43 [43, 42, 41.5] cm), ending with a WS row.

BO 5 (6, 7, 8) sts at beg of next 2 rows—32 (34, 34, 36) sts. Place rem sts on a holder.

Raglan Shaping

With RS facing, place all the pieces onto larger circular in this order: right front, place marker (pm), sleeve, pm, back, pm, sleeve, pm, left front—197 (209, 217, 229) sts. Work back and forth.

NEXT ROW (RAGLAN DEC ROW 1): *Knit to 3 sts before marker, ssk, k1, sl m, k1, k2tog; rep from * 3 more times, knit to end—8 sts dec'd.

NEXT ROW (WS): Knit.

Rep last 2 rows 2 (3, 3, 3) more times—173 (177, 185, 197) sts.

Knit 5 rows even.

NEXT ROW (RAGLAN DEC ROW 2): *Knit to 3 sts before marker, ssk, k1, sl m, knit sleeve sts, sl m, k1, k2tog; rep from * once more, knit to end—4 sts dec'd.

Knit 5 rows even.

NEXT ROW: Rep Raglan Dec Row 1—8 sts dec'd.

Rep last 12 rows once more.

Knit 5 rows even.

NEXT ROW: Rep Raglan Dec Row 2—4 sts dec'd.

Size L (XL) only:

Knit 5 rows even.

NEXT ROW: Rep Raglan Dec Row 1—8 sts dec'd.

All sizes:

Knit 5 (5, 3, 5) rows even.

NEXT ROW: Rep Raglan Dec Row 1—8 sts dec'd.

Knit 1 row even.

Rep last 2 rows 3 (3, 3, 4) more times, then rep Raglan Dec Row 1 once more—105 (109, 109, 113) sts rem.

Collar

Change to smaller needles.

NEXT ROW (DEC): K12 (14, 14, 16), *k2tog, k7; rep from * 9 times more,

knit to end—95 (99, 99, 103) sts. Cont even in garter st until collar measures 2" (5 cm). BO knitwise.

Finishing

Sew sleeve and side seams. Sew underarm seams. Weave in ends. Sew snaps to neck edge, so fronts overlap about 5" (12.5 cm).

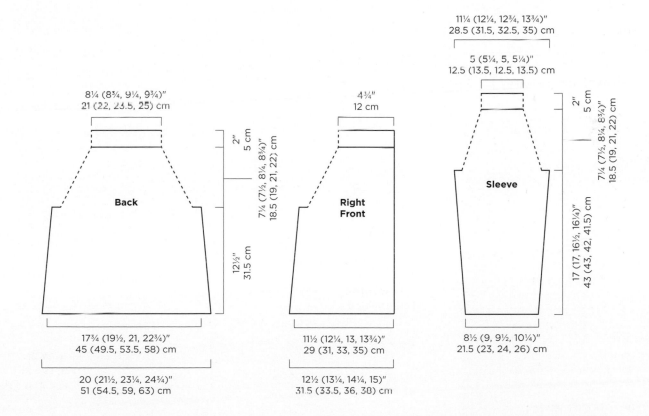

8¼ (8¾, 9¼, 9¾)"
21 (22, 23.5, 25) cm

2"
5 cm

7¼ (7½, 8¼, 8¾)"
18.5 (19, 21, 22) cm

Back

12½"
31.5 cm

17¾ (19½, 21, 22¾)"
45 (49.5, 53.5, 58) cm

20 (21½, 23¼, 24¾)"
51 (54.5, 59, 63) cm

4¾"
12 cm

Right Front

11½ (12¼, 13, 13¾)"
29 (31, 33, 35) cm

12½ (13¼, 14¼, 15)"
31.5 (33.5, 36, 38) cm

11¼ (12¼, 12¾, 13¾)"
28.5 (31.5, 32.5, 35) cm

5 (5¼, 5, 5¼)"
12.5 (13.5, 12.5, 13.5) cm

2"
5 cm

7¼ (7½, 8¼, 8¾)"
18.5 (19, 21, 22) cm

Sleeve

17 (17, 16½, 16¼)"
43 (43, 42, 41.5) cm

8½ (9, 9½, 10¼)"
21.5 (23, 24, 26) cm

Fiona
Garter Stitch Coat with Tucks

The tucks in this coat are made by knitting one stitch in the row below running all the way up from the lower edge—straight up the tuck. The coat is knitted with two different yarns that combine for a lovely, lofty texture: a fine and sturdy wool yarn plus a light and fluffy kid mohair and silk yarn.

		S	M	L	XL
BUST (BUTTONED)	in	33	36¼	39½	42½
	cm	84	92	100	108
LENGTH	in	31	32	32¾	33½
	cm	79	81	83	85

Yarn Fingering weight (Superfine #1). Shown in: Sandnes Garn Silk Mohair (60% kid mohair, 15% wool, 25% silk; 306 yd [280 m]/50 g); charcoal #1076, 4 (4, 5, 5) balls, and Sandnes Garn Sisu (80% wool, 20% nylon; 191 yd [175 m]/50 g); gray #1042, 7 (7, 8, 8) balls.

Needles U.S. size 10 (6 mm): straight and 32" (80 cm) circular (cir) needle. Adjust needle sizes if necessary to obtain the correct gauge. U.S. sizes 8 (5 mm): straight needles.

Notions Cable needle (cn), stitch markers (m), stitch holders, tapestry needle, and five ¾" (19 mm) buttons.

Gauge 15 sts and 28 rows = 4" (10 cm) in garter st with larger needles and 1 strand of each yarn held together.

Body

With larger cir needle, CO 171 (187, 199, 211) sts. Work back and forth; do not join.

SET-UP ROW (WS): Knit.

ROW 1: K23 (25, 26, 27), k1-b, k21 (23, 25, 27), place marker (pm), k28 (32, 35, 38), k1-b, k23, k1-b, k28 (32, 35, 38), pm, k21 (23, 25, 27), k1-b, k23 (25, 26, 27).

Cont in garter st and k1-b every RS row until piece measures 4 (3½, 3½, 3½)" (10 [9, 9, 9] cm), ending with a WS row.

NEXT ROW (DEC): *Knit to 3 sts before m, ssk, k2, k2tog; rep from * once more, knit to end—4 sts dec'd.

Rep dec row every 2¾ (2¼, 2¼, 2¼)" (7 [6, 6, 6] cm) 5 (6, 6, 6) times more—147 (159, 171, 183) sts rem. *At the same time,* make first buttonhole on a RS row when piece measures 11¾ (11¾, 12, 11¾)" (30 [30, 30.5, 30] cm), and work 4 rem buttonholes every 4 (4¼, 4¼, 4½)" (10 [11, 11, 11.5] cm).

When piece measures about 20 (20½, 20½, 21)" (51 [52, 52, 53.5] cm), end with a WS row.

NEXT (TUCK) ROW (RS): Work to 2 sts before k1-b, make Left Tuck, knit to 2 sts before next k1-b, make Left Tuck, k11, make Right Tuck, knit to 6 sts before last k1-b, make Right Tuck, knit to end—123 (135, 147, 159) sts.

Work even in garter st over all the sts for 1¼" (3 cm), ending with a WS row.

NEXT ROW (INC): *Knit to 1 st before m, M1, k2, M1; rep from * once more, knit to end—4 sts inc'd.

Rep inc row every 1¼" (3 cm) once more—131 (143, 155, 167) sts.

Work even until piece measures 23½ (24, 24¼, 24¾)" (60 [61, 61.5, 63] cm), ending with a WS row.

Divide for armholes

NEXT ROW (RS): Knit to 2 sts before marker, BO 2 sts for armhole, knit to marker, join a second ball of yarn, BO 2 sts for armhole, knit to end—61 (67, 73, 79) sts rem for back and 33 (36, 39, 42) sts rem for each front.

Place sts for each front on holders.

Back

BO 2 (2, 3, 3) sts at beg of next 2 rows, then 0 (2, 2, 2) sts at the beg of next 0 (2, 2, 4) rows—57 (59, 63, 65) sts.

Knit 1 row even.

STITCH GUIDE

K1-B *(knit one below)*

ROW 1 (RS): Insert the right needle into the row below the next stitch to be worked, knit and drop the stitch on the left needle.

ROW 2: Knit.

Repeat Rows 1–2.

LEFT TUCK
(tuck folds toward the left)

Worked over 9 stitches. Place the next 3 stitches on a cable needle and hold in front of work, place the next 3 stitches on a second cable needle. Arrange the two cable needles with the left needle at the back, the second cable needle in the center, and the first cable needle in front. *Knit the first stitch from each needle together*; repeat from * to * 2 times more, making sure to knit the last stitch of the top needle in the row below—6 stitches decreased.

RIGHT TUCK
(tuck folds toward the right)

Worked over 9 stitches. Place the next 3 stitches on a cable needle and hold in front of work, place the next 3 stitches on a second cable needle. Arrange the two cable needles with the left needle in the front, the second cable needle in the center, and the first cable needle at the back. *Knit the first stitch from each needle together*; repeat from * to * 2 times more, making sure to knit the first stitch of the top needle in the row below—6 stitches decreased.

BUTTONHOLES

Five buttonholes are worked along the right front edge. The buttonholes are spaced so the third buttonhole is worked at the top end of the tuck, and the top buttonhole is about ¾" (2 cm) below the beginning of neck shaping. Each buttonhole is worked on a RS row as follows: K3, BO 2, work to end. Next row, CO 2 new sts over the bind-off hole to complete the buttonhole.

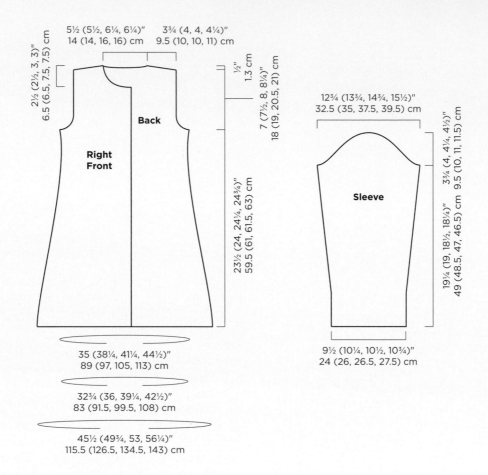

5½ (5½, 6¼, 6¼)"
14 (14, 16, 16) cm

3¾ (4, 4, 4¼)"
9.5 (10, 10, 11) cm

2½ (2½, 3, 3)"
6.5 (6.5, 7.5, 7.5) cm

Back

Right Front

½"
1.3 cm

7 (7½, 8, 8¼)"
18 (19, 20.5, 21) cm

23½ (24, 24¼, 24¾)"
59.5 (61, 61.5, 63) cm

35 (38¼, 41¼, 44½)"
89 (97, 105, 113) cm

32¾ (36, 39¼, 42½)"
83 (91.5, 99.5, 108) cm

45½ (49¾, 53, 56¼)"
115.5 (126.5, 134.5, 143) cm

12¾ (13¾, 14¾, 15½)"
32.5 (35, 37.5, 39.5) cm

Sleeve

3¾ (4, 4¼, 4½)"
9.5 (10, 11, 11.5) cm

19¼ (19, 18½, 18¼)"
49 (48.5, 47, 46.5) cm

9½ (10¼, 10½, 10¾)"
24 (26, 26.5, 27.5) cm

NEXT ROW: (RS, dec) K1, k2tog, knit to last 3 sts ssk, k1—2 sts dec'd.

Rep dec row every RS row 3 (3, 4, 4) times more—49 (51, 53, 55) sts rem.

Work even until armhole measures 7 (7½, 8, 8¼)" (18 [19, 20.5, 21] cm), ending with a WS row.

Shape neck and shoulders

NEXT ROW: BO 7 (7, 7, 8) sts, k7(8, 8, 8), place center 21 (21, 23, 23) sts on a holder for back neck, join a second ball of yarn and knit to end. Work each side separately.

NEXT ROW: BO 7 (7, 7, 8) sts, knit to end—7 (8, 8, 8) sts rem each side.

NEXT ROW: BO 7 (8, 8, 8) sts, knit to end.

NEXT ROW: BO rem 7 (8, 8, 8) sts.

Left Front

Place sts for left front on needles.

BO at beg of RS rows 2 (2, 3, 3) sts once, then 0 (2, 2, 2) sts 0 (1, 1, 2) time(s)—31 (32, 34, 35) sts.

Work 1 row even.

NEXT ROW: (RS, dec) K1, k2tog, knit to end—1 st dec'd.

Rep dec row every RS row 3 (3, 4, 4) times more—27 (28, 29, 30) sts rem.

Work even until armhole measures 5 (5½, 5½, 5¾)" (12.5 [14, 14, 14.5] cm), ending with a RS row.

Shape neck

NEXT ROW: BO 3 sts, k5 (5, 6, 6) and place on holder, knit to end—19 (20, 20, 21) sts.

BO at beg of WS rows 2 sts once, then 1 st 3 times—14 (15, 15, 16) sts.

Work even until armhole measures 7 (7½, 8, 8¼)" 18 [19, 20.5, 21] cm), ending with a WS row.

Shape shoulder

BO at beg of RS rows 7 sts 2 (1, 1, 0) time(s), then 8 sts 0 (1, 1, 2) time(s).

Right Front

Place sts for right front on needles and join yarn to beg with a WS row.

BO at beg of WS rows 2 (2, 3, 3) sts once, then 0 (2, 2, 2) sts 0 (1, 1, 2) time(s)—31 (32, 34, 35) sts.

NEXT ROW: (RS, dec) Knit to last 3 sts, ssk, k1—1 st dec'd.

Rep dec row every RS row 3 (3, 4, 4) times more—27 (28, 29, 30) sts rem.

Work even until armhole measures 5 (5½, 5½, 5¾)" (12.5 [14, 14, 14.5] cm), ending with a WS row.

Shape neck

NEXT ROW: BO 3 sts, k5 (5, 6, 6) and place on holder, knit to end—19 (20, 20, 21) sts.

BO at beg of RS rows 2 sts once, then 1 st 3 times—14 (15, 15, 16) sts.

Work even until armhole measures 7 (7½, 8, 8¼)" 18 [19, 20.5, 21] cm), ending with a RS row.

Shape shoulder

BO at beg of WS rows 7 sts 2 (1, 1, 0) time(s), then 8 sts 0 (1, 1, 2) time(s).

Sleeves

With larger needles, CO 36 (38, 39, 40) sts.

Work in garter st until piece measures 4" (10 cm), ending with a WS row.

NEXT ROW (RS, INC): K1, M1, knit to last st, M1, k1—2 sts inc'd.

Rep inc row 5 (6, 7, 8) times more on RS rows every 2¾ (2¼, 2, 1½)" (7 [6, 5, 4] cm)—48 (52, 55, 58) sts.

Work even until piece measures 19¼ (19, 18½, 18)" (49 [48, 47, 46] cm), ending with a RS row.

Shape sleeve cap

BO 3 sts at beg of next 2 rows, and 2 sts at beg of next 4 rows—34 (38, 41, 44) sts.

Knit 1 row even.

NEXT ROW (RS, DEC): K1, k2tog, knit to last 3 sts, ssk, k1—2 sts dec'd.

Rep dec row every RS row 6 (7, 8, 9) times more—20 (22, 23, 24) sts.

BO 2 sts at beg of next 2 rows, and 3 sts at beg of next 4 rows—4 (6, 7, 8) sts. BO rem sts.

Finishing

Weave in ends. Sew shoulder seams.

Collar

With smaller needles and RS facing, beg at holder on right front neck, k5 (5, 6, 6) from holder, pick up and k17 sts along right neck edge, k21 (21, 23, 23) sts from back neck holder, pick up and k17 sts along left neck edge, and k5 (5, 6, 6) from holder at left front neck—65 (65, 69, 69) sts.

Work in garter st until collar measures 1½" (4 cm).

NEXT ROW (INC): *K13 (13, 14, 14), M1; rep from * 3 times more, knit to end—69 (69, 73, 73) sts.

Work even until the collar measures about 3½" (9 cm). BO all sts.

Sew sleeve seams; seam the bottom 1¼-1½" (3-4 cm) with seam on RS so that you can turn up the cuff. Sew in sleeves. Sew buttons to left front opposite buttonholes.

Siri
Flattering Vintage Style

This shrug is knitted in a T shape, folded, and then sewn together to make a tube with holes for the arms. The elasticity of the garter ridges helps the shrug fit well. In spite of the simple shaping, it looks good on many different figure types.

		S	M	L	XL
WIDTH	in	14¼	14½	15	15¼
	cm	36	37	38	39
LENGTH	in	26¾	27	27½	27¾
	cm	68	68.5	70	70.5

Yarn DK weight (Light #3). Shown in: Sandnes Garn Alpaca (100% baby alpaca; 120 yd [110 m]/50 g); light blue #6211, 8 (9, 9, 10) balls.

Needles U.S. size 4 (3.5 mm): circular 32" (80 cm). Adjust needle size if necessary to obtain the correct gauge.

Notions Tapestry needle.

Gauge 21 sts and 54 rows = 4" (10 cm) in welt pattern.

notes:

A circular needle is used to accommodate the large number of stitches. Work back and forth and do not join.

When measuring, do not stretch the work but make sure the welts are relaxed.

STITCH GUIDE

WELT PATTERN
(over any number of sts)

ROW 1 (WS): Purl.

ROW 2: Knit.

ROW 3: Knit.

ROW 4: Purl.

ROW 5: Knit.

ROW 6: Knit.

Repeat Rows 1–6 for patt.

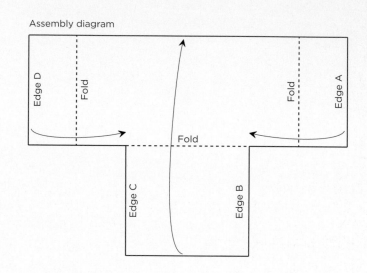

Assembly diagram

Shrug

CO 70 (71, 72, 73) sts (Edge A on the diagram).

Work in Welt patt until piece measures 11¾ (13, 14¼, 15¼)" (30 [33, 36, 39] cm), ending with patt Row 6. At the end of last row, CO 70 (71, 72, 73) sts—140 (142, 144, 146) sts (Edge B on the diagram).

Cont even in welt patt for 14¼ (14½, 15, 15¼)" (36 [37, 38, 39] cm), ending with patt Row 6.

NEXT ROW (WS): BO 70 (71, 72, 73) sts, work to end—70 (71, 72, 73) sts rem (Edge C on the diagram).

Cont even for 11¾ (13, 14¼, 15¼)" (30 [33, 36, 39] cm), ending with patt Row 1. BO all sts knitwise (Edge D on the diagram).

Finishing

Weave in ends.

Assembly

Lay piece flat with narrow portion at the bottom, forming a "T." Fold the bottom half up as shown in the assembly diagram. Fold Edge A toward center along the fold line as shown, so that Edges A and B meet. With RS facing, use mattress stitch to join edges A and B, leaving 6 (6½, 7, 7¾)" (15 [16.5, 18, 19.5] cm) open along long edge for armhole. Rep with Edges C and D.

Tara
Scarf with Lace Edging

This scarf is knitted diagonally with a lace edging on both sides. It is wider at the center than at the ends, without being definitely triangular, and is perfect for winding around your neck numerous times. This sample was knit with a super soft alpaca and Merino wool yarn but other yarns can easily be substituted.

		before blocking	after blocking
WIDTH AT CENTER	in	11	11
	cm	28	28
LENGTH	in	59	63
	cm	150	160

note:

The scarf is worked from point to point with a narrow lace edging along the straight side and both lace and fagoting along the diagonal sides.

Yarn Fingering weight (Superfine #1). Shown in: Isager Alpaca 2 (50% alpaca, 50% merino wool; 547 yd [500 m]/100 g): yellow-green #112, 2 skeins.

Needles U.S. size 6 (4 mm) needles. Adjust needle size if necessary to obtain the correct gauge.

Notions Locking markers (m) or safety pins, tapestry needle.

Gauge 25 sts and 44½ rows = 4" (10 cm) in garter st.

Scarf

CO 5 sts.

ROW 1: K1, yo, k1, yo, k2, yo twice, k1—9 sts.

ROW 2: K2, k1-tbl, k2, yo, k2, yo, k2—10 sts.

ROW 3: K3, yo, k2tog, k1, yo, k2tog, k3—11 sts.

ROW 4: BO 2 (1 st rem on right needle), k2, yo, k2tog, k1, yo, k2tog, k1—9 sts.

ROW 5: K3, yo, k2tog, k1, yo, k2, (yo) twice, k1—12 sts.

ROW 6: K2, k1-tbl, k3, yo, k2tog, k1, yo, k2tog, k1.

ROW 7: K3, yo, k2tog, k1, yo, k2tog, k1, k3.

ROW 8: BO 2 (1 st rem on right needle), k3, yo, k2tog, k1, yo, k2tog, k1—10 sts.

ROW 9: K3, yo, k2tog, k1, yo, k2tog, k1, (yo) twice, k1—12 sts.

ROW 10: K2, k1-tbl, k3, yo, k3, yo, k2tog, k1—13 sts.

ROW 11: K3, yo, k2tog, k2, yo, k2tog, k1, k3.

ROW 12: BO 2 (1 st rem on right needle), k3, yo, k2tog, k2, yo, k2tog, k1—11 sts.

ROW 13: K3, yo, k2tog, k2, yo, k2tog, k1, (yo) twice, k1—13 sts.

ROW 14: K2, k1-tbl, k3, yo, k2tog, M1, k2, yo, k2tog, k1—14 sts.

ROW 15: K3, yo, k2tog, knit to last 6 sts, yo, k2tog, k4.

ROW 16: BO 2 (1 st rem on right needle), k3, yo, k2tog, knit to last 3 sts, yo, k2tog, k1—2 sts dec'd.

ROW 17: K3, yo, k2tog, knit to last 4 sts, yo, k2tog, k1, (yo) twice, k1—2 sts inc'd.

ROW 18: K2, k1-tbl, k3, yo, k2tog, M1, knit to last 3 sts, yo, k2tog, k1—1 st inc'd.

Rep Rows 15–18 twenty-eight times—40 sts, plus 3 lace edging sts. Place marker (pm) in straight edge.

ROW 131: K3, yo, knit to last 6 sts, yo, k2tog, k4.

ROW 132: BO 2 (1 st rem on right needle), k3, yo, k2tog, knit to last 3 sts, yo, k2tog, k1—2 sts dec'd.

ROW 133: K3, yo, k2tog, knit to last 4 sts, yo, k2tog, k1, (yo) twice, k1—2 sts inc'd.

ROW 134: K2, k1-tbl, k3, yo, k2tog, knit to last 3 sts, yo, k2tog, k1.

ROW 135: K3, yo, k2tog, knit to last 6 sts, yo, k2tog, k4.

ROW 136: BO 2 (1 st rem on right needle), k3, yo, k2tog, M1, knit to last 3 sts, yo, k2tog, k1—1 st dec'd.

ROW 137: K3, yo, k2tog, knit to last 4 sts, yo, k2tog, k1, (yo) twice, k2—2 sts inc'd.

ROW 138: K2, k1-tbl, k3, yo, k2tog, knit to last 3 sts, yo, k2tog, k1.

ROW 139: K3, yo, k2tog, knit to last 6 sts, yo, k2tog, k4.

ROW 140: BO 2 (1 st rem on right needle), k3, yo, k2tog, knit to last 3 sts, yo, k2tog, k1—2 sts dec'd.

ROW 141: K3, yo, k2tog, knit to last 4 sts, yo, k2tog, (yo) twice, k1—2 sts inc'd.

ROW 142: K2, k1-tbl, k3, yo, k2tog, M1, knit to last 3 sts, yo, k2tog, k1—1 st inc'd.

Rep Rows 131–142 fourteen more times—73 sts.

ROW 311: K3, yo, knit to last 6 sts, yo, k2tog, k4.

ROW 312: BO 2 (1 st rem on right needle), k3, yo, k2tog, knit to last 3 sts, yo, k2tog, k1—2 sts dec'd.

ROW 313: K3, yo, k2tog, knit to last 4 sts, yo, k2tog, k1, (yo) twice, k1—2 sts inc'd.

ROW 314: K2, k1-tbl, k3, yo, k2tog, knit to last 3 sts, yo, k2tog, k1.

Rep Rows 311–314 eight more times; piece should measure about 31" (79 cm). Pm in straight edge 1½" (4 cm) down from needle for center.

ROW 347: K3, yo, k2tog, knit to last 6 sts, yo, k2tog, k4.

ROW 348: BO 2 (1 st rem on right needle), k3, yo, k2tog, knit to last 3 sts, yo, k2tog, k1—2 sts dec'd.

ROW 349: K3, yo, k2tog, knit to last 4 sts, yo, k2tog, k1, (yo) twice, k1—2 sts inc'd.

ROW 350: K2, k1-tbl, k3, yo, k2tog, knit to last 3 sts, yo, k2tog, k1.

ROW 351: K3, yo, k2tog, knit to last 6 sts, yo, k2tog, k4.

ROW 352: BO 2 (1 st rem on right needle), k3, yo, (k2tog) twice, knit to last 3 sts, yo, k2tog, k1—3 sts dec'd.

ROW 353: K3, yo, k2tog, knit to last 4 sts, yo, k2tog, k1, (yo) twice, k2—2 sts inc'd.

ROW 354: K2, k1-tbl, k3, yo, k2tog, knit to last 3 sts, yo, k2tog, k1.

ROW 355: K3, yo, k2tog, knit to last 6 sts, yo, k2tog, k4.

ROW 356: BO 2 (1 st rem on right needle), k3, yo, k2tog, knit to last 3 sts, yo, k2tog, k1—2 sts dec'd.

ROW 357: K3, yo, k2tog, knit to last 4 sts, yo, k2tog, (yo) twice, k1—2 sts inc'd.

ROW 358: K2, k1-tbl, k3, yo, (k2tog) twice, knit to last 3 sts, yo, k2tog, k1—1 st dec'd.

Rep Rows 347–358 fourteen more times—43 sts.

ROW 527: K3, yo, k2tog, knit to last 6 sts, yo, k2tog, k4.

ROW 528: BO 2 (1 st rem on right needle), k3, yo, k2tog, knit to last 3 sts, yo, k2tog, k1—2 sts dec'd.

ROW 529: K3, yo, k2tog, knit to last 4 sts, yo, k2tog, k1, (yo) twice, k1—2 sts inc'd

ROW 530: K2, k1-tbl, k3, yo, (k2tog) twice, knit to last 3 sts, yo, k2tog, k1—1 st dec'd.

Rep Rows 527–530 twenty-nine more times, then rep Rows 527 and 528 once more—11 sts.

ROW 649: K3, yo, k3tog, k1, yo, k2tog, k1, (yo) twice, k1—12 sts.

ROW 650: K2, k1-tbl, k3, yo, k2tog, k1, yo, k2tog, k1.

ROW 651: K3, yo, sk2p, yo, k2tog, k4—11 sts.

ROW 652: BO 2 (1 st rem on right needle), k5, yo, k2tog, k1—9 sts.

ROW 653: K3, yo, k3tog, yo, k2, (yo) twice, k1—11 sts.

ROW 654: K2, k1-tbl, k5, yo, k2tog, k1.

ROW 655: K3, yo, k3tog, k2tog, k3—9 sts.

ROW 656: BO 2 (1 st rem on right needle), k3, yo, k2tog, k1—7 sts.

ROW 657: K2tog, k1, yo, k2tog, k1, (yo) twice, k1—8 sts.

ROW 658: K2, k1-tbl, k3, k2tog—7 sts.

ROW 659: K2tog, yo, k5.

BO rem sts.

Finishing

Weave in ends, gathering tips of scarf slightly so that they are smooth. Wet-block, spin out excess water, and block to finished measurements.

Rosita
Long Garter Stitch Sweater

This long sweater is worked from side to side, for a dramatic look. The shapely and becoming A-line sweater is accentuated by numerous gores on the lower section that open up through short-rows within the stockinette stripes.

		S	M	L	XL
BUST	in	38	42	46	49
	cm	96.5	106.5	117	124.5
LENGTH	in	30¼	30¾	31½	32
	cm	77	78	80	81

Yarn DK weight (Light #3). Shown in: BC Garn Semilla Fino (100% organic wool; 175 yd [160 m]/50 g): beige #103, 11 (11, 12, 14) balls.

Needles U.S. size 1.5 (2.5 mm): 32" (80 cm) circular (cir). U.S. size 4 (3.5 mm): 32" (80 cm) circular. Adjust needle sizes if necessary to obtain the correct gauge.

Notions Stitch markers (m), contrast color waste yarn for provisional CO, stitch holders, nine ¾" (19 mm) leather buttons.

Gauge 24 sts and 54 rows = 4" (10 cm) in stripe patt on larger needles.

notes:

The body of this sweater begins with a provisional cast-on at the right-hand side of the back and is worked first across the back and then the left front. Remove the provisional cast-on and then work the right front from those stitches.

Lightly smooth out the pieces when you measure them, being careful not to stretch the work.

Short-rows are used to shape the back and front pieces. When working across rows with wrapped stitches, make sure to pick up the wrap and work it together with the stitch it wraps.

Tighten the first and last stitch of every knit row for a firmer and more even edge.

Stitch Guide

STRIPE PATTERN

*4 rows reverse St st, 6 rows St st; repeat from * for patt.

SHORT-ROWS

To avoid holes when turning and to make them less visible, wrap yarn around the turned stitch as follows: slip the last st before turning over to the right needle. Bring yarn in front of work and move slipped st back to the left needle. Turn and work back.

Back

With larger needle and scrap yarn, provisionally CO 134 (133, 132, 131) sts. Join Semilla Fino. Work 4 rows in St st. **Beg stripe pattern and *at the same time,* beg raglan shaping and short-row shaping as foll:

Raglan shaping

At the beg of the 2nd (3rd, 3rd, 4th) reverse St st stripe, inc (1 st at the end of next WS row, 2 sts at end of next WS row) 15 (16, 18, 19) times—179 (181, 186, 188) sts.

Short-Rows

When there are 4 (4, 4, 5) reverse St st stripes, cont as foll on the next St st stripe: Knit 1 row.

SHORT-ROW 1 (WS): P35, w&t.

SHORT-ROW 2: Knit to bottom edge.

SHORT-ROW 3: Purl to 3 sts past previous turn, w&t.

SHORT-ROW 4: Knit to bottom edge.

Rep Short-Rows 3 and 4 once more.

Work 5 rows of St st, then 4 rows of reverse St st over all the sts, ending with a WS row.

*Knit 1 row.

SHORT-ROW 5 (WS): Purl to 5 sts past previous turn, w&t.

SHORT-ROW 6: Knit to bottom edge.

SHORT-ROW 7: Purl to 3 sts past previous turn, w&t.

Rep Short-Rows 6 and 7 once more, then rep Short-Row 6 once more.

Work 5 rows of St st, then 4 rows of reverse St st over all the sts.* Rep from * to * 7 (7, 8, 8) more times; short-rows should move higher up the back each time. When raglan inc are complete, place marker (pm) at the last raglan inc and cont rem short-rows as est. When last 16-row short-row rep is complete, piece should measure about 9½ (10½, 11½, 12¼)" (24 [26.5, 29, 31] cm) from cast-on at armhole, and short-rows should be about 7¾" (20 cm) below back neck edge. Lightly smooth out garment when you measure it but do not stretch it or the finished garment will be too small. Pm at neck edge 2 rows below needle for center of neck.

Work 5 rows of St st.

SHORT-ROW 8 (WS): Purl to where last short-row was turned, w&t.

SHORT-ROW 9: Knit to bottom edge.

SHORT-ROW 10: Purl to 3 sts before previous turn, w&t.

Rep Short-Rows 9 and 10 once more, then rep Short-Row 9 once more.

Purl 1 row over all sts. Work 4 rows of reverse St st, ending with a WS row.

*Work 5 rows of St st.

SHORT-ROW 11: (WS) Purl to 5 sts before previous turn, w&t.

SHORT-ROW 12: Knit back to bottom edge.

SHORT-ROW 13: Purl to 3 sts before previous turn, w&t.

Rep Short-Rows 12 and 13 once more, then rep Short-Row 12 once more. Purl 1 row over all the sts.

Work 4 rows of reverse St st*. Rep from * to * 8 (8, 9, 9) times more. *At the same time,* when the same number of St st and reverse St st stripes have been worked on second half of back neck as for first half, shape raglan as foll:

BO (2 sts at beg of next RS row, then 1 st at the beg of next RS row) 15 (16, 18, 19) times—134 (133, 132, 131) sts rem.

Work even in pattern without further shaping until piece ends with same number of stripes as beg of back, ending with 4 rows of St st. Do not bind off.

Left Front

Work 2 rows of St st. Pm at the center of these 6 rows (= left side seam). Work as for back from ** until all the raglan increases have been made—179 (181, 186, 188) sts. Pm at last raglan inc. Cont short-rows as est and *at the same time*, shape front neck as foll:

Shape neck

BO at beg of RS rows 6 sts once, 3 sts once, 2 sts once, and 1 st 4 times—164 (166, 171, 173) sts.

Work even until 9 (9, 10, 10) sets of short-rows have been completed, ending with 5 rows of St st. Place sts on holders or scrap yarn.

Right Front

Remove the provisional cast-on and place live sts on larger needle.

Work 2 rows of St st. Pm at the center of these 6 rows (= right side seam).

Beg stripe pattern and *at the same time*, beg raglan shaping and short-row shaping as foll:

Raglan shaping

At the beg of the 2nd (3rd, 3rd, 4th) reverse St st stripe, inc (1 st at the beg of next WS row, 2 sts at beg of next WS row) 15 (16, 18, 19) times—179 (181, 186, 188) sts.

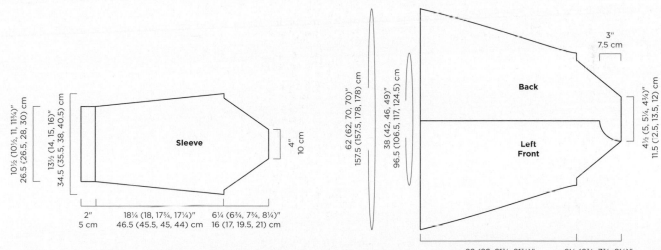

Sleeve

10½ (10½, 11, 11¾)"
26.5 (26.5, 28, 30) cm

13½ (14, 15, 16)"
34.5 (35.5, 38, 40.5) cm

4"
10 cm

2"
5 cm

18¼ (18, 17¾, 17¼)"
46.5 (45.5, 45, 44) cm

6¼ (6¾, 7¾, 8¼)"
16 (17, 19.5, 21) cm

Back

Left Front

3"
7.5 cm

62 (62, 70, 70)"
157.5 (157.5, 178, 178) cm

38 (42, 46, 49)"
96.5 (106.5, 117, 124.5) cm

4½ (5, 5¼, 4¾)"
11.5 (12.5, 13.5, 12) cm

22 (22, 21¾, 21¾)"
56 (56, 55, 55) cm

6¼ (6¾, 7¾, 8¼)"
16 (17, 19.5, 21) cm

Short-Rows

When there are 4 (4, 4, 5) reverse St st stripes, cont as foll on the next St st stripe:

SHORT-ROW 1 (RS): K35, w&t.

SHORT-ROW 2: Purl to bottom edge.

SHORT-ROW 3: Knit to 3 sts past previous turn, w&t.

SHORT-ROW 4: Purl to bottom edge.

Rep Short-Rows 3 and 4 once more.

Work 5 rows of St st, then 4 rows of reverse St st over all the sts, ending with a RS row.

*Purl 1 row.

SHORT-ROW 5 (RS): Knit to 5 sts past previous turn, w&t.

SHORT-ROW 6: Purl to bottom edge.

SHORT-ROW 7: Knit to 3 sts past previous turn, w&t.

Rep Short-Rows 6 and 7 once more, then rep Short-Row 6 once more.

Work 5 rows of St st, then 4 rows of reverse St st over all the sts.* Rep from * to * 7 (7, 8, 8) times more. When raglan inc are complete, place marker (pm) at the last raglan inc.

Cont rem short-rows as est and *at the same time,* shape neck as foll:

Shape neck

BO at beg of WS rows 6 sts once, 3 sts once, 2 sts once, and 1 st 4 times—164 (166, 171, 173) sts.

Work even until 9 (9, 10, 10) sets of short-rows have been completed, ending with 5 rows of St st. Place sts on holders or scrap yarn.

Sleeves

With larger needles, CO 19 (24, 26, 19) sts. Work 4 rows of St st.

Cont in stripe pattern and *at the same time,* CO 7 (6, 5, 5) sts at the end of every RS row 13 (14, 16, 17) times, make sure to CO loosely so edge won't pull in. *At the same time,* at the beg of 2nd (3rd, 3rd, 4th) reverse St st, beg raglan shaping as foll:

Inc (1 st at the end of next WS row, 2 sts at end of next WS row) 15 (16, 18, 19) times—155 (156, 160, 161) sts when all inc is complete. Pm after last raglan inc.

Work even until sleeve measures about 6¾ (7, 7½, 8)" (17 [18, 19, 20.5] cm) from beg, ending with a reverse St st stripe. Pm at center of this stripe (= center of sleeve).

Work even until the same number of St st and reverse St st stripes have been worked on second half of sleeve cap as for first half, shape raglan as foll:

BO (2 sts at beg of next RS row, then 1 st at the beg of next RS row) 15 (16, 18, 19) times and *at the same time,* when the same number of St st and reverse St st stripes have been worked on second half of bottom of sleeve as for first half, shape underarm as foll:

BO 7 (6, 5, 5) sts at the beg of every WS row 13 (14, 16, 17) times, ending with 4 rows of St st—19 (24, 26, 19) sts rem. BO rem sts.

Cuff

With smaller cir needle and RS facing, pick up and knit 3 sts in every St st stripe and 2 sts in every reverse St st stripe along lower edge of sleeve—about 82 (84, 88, 92) sts. Work even in garter st for 2" (5 cm) or until sleeve is desired length. BO all sts.

Finishing

Sew sleeve seam. Sew raglan seams, matching markers on sleeves to markers on front and back.

Collar

With smaller needles and RS facing, pick up and k30 (35, 40, 45) sts along right neck edge, 23 sts along right sleeve edge, 40 sts along back neck edge, 23 sts along left sleeve edge, and 30 (35, 40, 45) sts along left neck edge—146 (156, 166, 176) sts.

NEXT ROW (WS): Knit and dec 16 (22, 28, 34) sts evenly spaced across row—130 (134, 138, 142) sts.

Work even in garter st until collar measures about 3¼" (8 cm). Work in St st for 3¼" (8 cm). BO all sts.

Fold the St st section to WS and sew to neck edge.

Front bands

Return held sts for left front to smaller cir needle. Join yarn at lower edge and knit, pick up and k20 sts along left collar edge—184 (186, 191, 193) sts. Work in garter st for 1½" (3.5 cm), ending with a RS row. BO all sts knitwise.

With smaller needle and RS facing, pick up and k20 sts along right collar edge, return held sts to needle and knit across—184 (186, 191, 193) sts.

Work in garter st for ¾" (2 cm), ending with a WS row.

BUTTONHOLE ROW (RS): K30 (32, 37, 39), *BO 3 for buttonhole, k16; rep from * 6 times more, BO 3 for buttonhole, k12, BO 3 for buttonhole, k3.

NEXT ROW: CO 3 sts over gap left at each bind-off. Work even in garter st until band measures 1½" (3.5 cm), ending with a RS row. BO all sts knitwise.

Sew on buttons to left band opposite buttonholes.

Leaf
Patterns

It is fascinating that fine leaf shapes can be made with simple increases and decreases. The leaves float prettily above a background of purl stitches. The increases in the leaves are made with yarnovers, increases that also shape the knitted garment. For example, in a vest and cap, the piece widens as the leaves unfold.

Palma
Detail Features on Both Front and Back

This top has a lovely construction: it begins with a long, wide rib that forms the front and collar. The back is knit next with a pretty leaf motif branching out down the center. The sleeves are next, and, finally, there is a wide ribbed band at the waist. The lovely silk and wool blend yarn gives the top a beautiful drape.

		S	M	L	XL
WIDTH	in	33	35½	38½	41¾
	cm	84	90	98	106
LENGTH	in	20	20¾	21¾	22¾
	cm	51	52.5	55	57

Yarn Sportweight (Fine #2). Shown in: BC Garn Silkbloom Fino (55% merino wool, 45% silk; 218 yd [200 m]/50 g): lavender ix17, 5 (6, 6, 7) balls.

Needles U.S. size 4 (3.5 mm): 32" (80 cm) circular (cir) needle. Adjust needle sizes if necessary to obtain the correct gauge. U.S. size 2.5 (3 mm): 24" (60 cm) circular needle.

Notions Cable needle (cn), stitch holders, tapestry needle.

Gauge 25 sts and 36 rows = 4" (10 cm) in St st on larger needles; 27 sts and 39 rows = 4" (10 cm) in Back Chart pattern on larger needles.

notes:

The sweater is begun by working the collar, then working the cable panel down the back. The sides of the body and sleeves are worked by picking up stitches along the side of the cable panel and working them along with stitches along one side of the collar. After seaming the side and underarm edges, overlap the collar and pick up stitches along the end of the collar and lower edge of the body.

Stitch Guide

1/1 LC *(1 over 1 left cross)*
Sl 1 st to cn and hold in front, k1, k1 from cn.

1/1 LPC *(1 over 1 left purl cross)*
Sl 1 st to cn and hold in front, p1, k1 from cn.

1/1 RC *(1 over 1 right cross)*
Sl 1 st to cn and hold in back, k1, k1 from cn.

1/1 RPC *(1 over 1 right purl cross)*
Sl 1 st to cn and hold in back, k1, p1 from cn.

1/2 LPC *(1 over 2 left purl cross)*
Sl 1 st to cn and hold in front, p2, k1 from cn.

1/2 RPC *(1 over 2 right purl cross)*
Sl 2 sts to cn and hold in back, k1, p2 from cn.

2/1 LPC *(2 over 1 left purl cross)*
Sl 2 sts to cn and hold in front, p1, k2 from cn.

2/1 RPC *(2 over 1 right purl cross)*
Sl 1 st to cn and hold in back, k2, p1 from cn.

3/1 LPC *(3 over 1 left purl cross)*
Sl 3 sts to cn and hold in front, p1, k3 from cn.

3/1 RPC *(3 over 1 right purl cross)*
Sl 1 st to cn and hold in back, k3, p1 from cn.

3/2 LPC *(3 over 2 left purl cross)*
Sl 3 sts to cn and hold in front, p2, k3 from cn.

3/2 RPC *(3 over 2 right purl cross)*
Sl 2 sts to cn and hold in back, k3, p2 from cn.

4/4 LC *(4 over 4 left cross)*
Sl 4 sts to cn and hold in front, k4, k4 from cn.

Collar

With larger cir needle, CO 269 (281, 293, 305) sts. Work back and forth in rib as foll:

ROW 1 (WS): K1 (edge st), p3, *k3, p3; rep from * to last st, k1 (edge st).

ROW 2: K1 (edge st), *k3, p3; rep from * to last 3 sts, k3, k1 (edge st).

Rep Rows 1 and 2 until piece measures 9½" (24 cm), ending with a RS row.

NEXT ROW: Work 103 (109, 115, 121) sts in rib and place on holder for left front, work center 63 sts in rib, place rem 103 (109, 115, 121) sts on holder for right front.

Back

ROW 1 (RS): M1 in strand between held sts and first st on needle, work Row 1 of Back Chart (see page 42) across 63 sts and inc 4 sts as indicated on chart, M1 in strand between last st and held sts—69 sts.

ROW 2: K1 (edge st), work Row 2 of Back Chart to last st, k1 (edge st).

Work through Row 58, then rep Rows 3–58, keeping edge sts in garter st (knit every row) until back measures 11¾ (12½, 13½, 14¼)" (30 [32, 34, 36] cm), ending with a RS row and dec first and last st on last row—67 sts. *Note:* Do not begin a new leaf if it cannot be completed; instead, work those sts in reverse St st. Place rem sts on st holder.

Right Sleeve

With larger cir needle and RS facing, pick up and knit 75 (81, 87, 93) sts along right side edge of back, purl 103 (109,115, 121) held collar sts and, *at the same time,* dec 10 (12, 12, 12) sts evenly spaced over these sts, dec only over purl sts—168 (178, 190, 202) sts.

Work even in reverse St st for 1¾ (2¼, 3¼, 4)" (4.5 [6, 8, 10] cm).

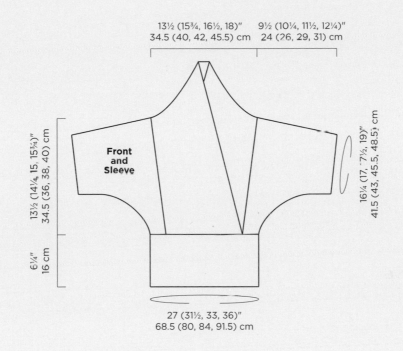

13½ (15¾, 16½, 18)"
34.5 (40, 42, 45.5) cm

9½ (10¼, 11½, 12¼)"
24 (26, 29, 31) cm

Front and Sleeve

13½ (14¼, 15, 15¾)"
34.5 (36, 38, 40) cm

6¼"
16 cm

16¼ (17, 7½, 19)"
41.5 (43, 45.5, 48.5) cm

27 (31½, 33, 36)"
68.5 (80, 84, 91.5) cm

Shape Sides

BO 6 (9, 12, 14) sts at beg of next 2 rows—156 (160, 166, 174) sts. BO 2 sts at beg of next 18 rows, then 1 st at beg of next 18 (18, 20, 20) rows—102 (106, 110, 118) sts rem.

Work even for ¾ (¾, 1¼, 1¼)" (2 [2, 3, 3] cm) and inc 14 (10, 12, 10) sts evenly spaced across last row, ending with a WS row—116 (116, 122, 128) sts.

Change to smaller cir needle.

NEXT ROW (RS): K1 (edge st), *k3, p3; rep from * to last st, k1 (edge st).

NEXT ROW: K1 (edge st), *k3, p3; rep from * to last st, k1 (edge st).

Continue as est until rib measures 2¾" (7 cm). BO in ribbing.

Left Sleeve

With larger cir needle and RS facing, purl 103 (109, 115, 121) held collar sts and, *at the same time,* dec 10 (12, 12, 12) sts evenly spaced over these sts, dec only over purl sts, then pick up and knit 75 (81, 87, 93) sts along rem side of the back—168 (178, 190, 202) sts.

Work left sleeve same as right.

Finishing

Sew sleeve and side seams.

Bottom band

Overlap the front pieces/ribbing with the right front on top. With smaller cir needle and RS facing, beg with held sts for back, k3, p2, k2tog, k6, ssk, p2, k3, work next next 27 sts in next row of chart, k3, p2, k2tog, k6, ssk, p2, k3, pick up and knit 30 (33, 39, 45) sts along edge to collar, 63 sts along edge of both layers of collar, and 30 (33, 39, 45) sts along rem edge—186 (192, 204, 216) sts. Join to work in the rnd. Pm for beg of rnd.

Purl 1 rnd. Continue in k3, p3 rib for 6¼" (16 cm). BO loosely in ribbing.

Back Chart

57
55
53
51
49
47
45
43
41
39
37
35
33
31
29
27
25
23
21
19
17
15
13
11
9
7
5
3
1
67 sts (excluding leaves)

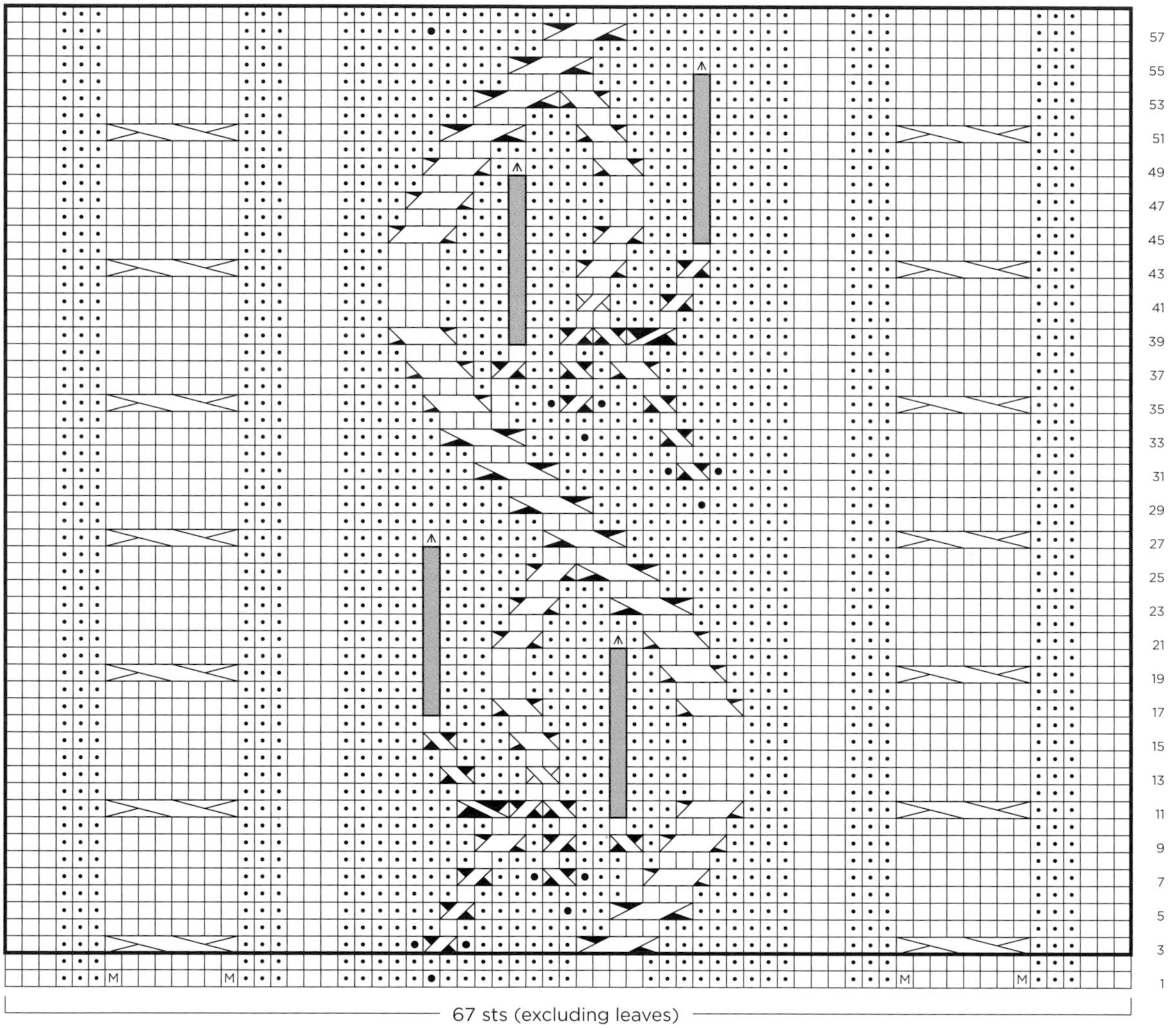

Leaf Insert Chart

9
7
5
3
1

	k on RS; p on WS
•	p on RS; k on WS
\	ssk
/	k2tog
ʌ	sl 2 as if to k2tog, k1, psso
•	bobble = (k1, yo, k1, yo, k1) in same st, turn; p5, turn; sl sts 2–5 over first st, k-tbl of rem st
M	make 1
⌁	kf&b in strand between sts
⤬	1/1 RC (see Stitch Guide)
⤬	1/1 LC (see Stitch Guide)
⤬	1/1 RPC (see Stitch Guide)
⤬	1/1 LPC (see Stitch Guide)
⤬	1/2 LPC (see Stitch Guide)
⤬	1/2 RPC (see Stitch Guide)
⤬	2/1 RPC (see Stitch Guide)
⤬	2/1 LPC (see Stitch Guide)
⤬	3/1 RPC (see Stitch Guide)
⤬	3/1 LPC (see Stitch Guide)
⤬	3/2 RPC (see Stitch Guide)
⤬	3/2 LPC (see Stitch Guide)
⤬	4/4 LC (see Stitch Guide)
■	work Leaf Insert Chart
□	pattern repeat

Lily
The Softest Leaf

In this garment the leaf pattern on the yoke really floats above the garter-ridge background. If you are impatient about finishing, then this sweater is for you: the front bands and buttonholes are worked at the same time as the fronts so the sweater just has to be seamed.

		S	M	L	XL
WIDTH	in	34¼	39½	42½	46
	cm	87	100.5	108	117
LENGTH	in	18¾	19½	20	20½
	cm	47.5	49.5	51	52

Yarn Worsted weight (Medium #4). Shown in: Onion Camel + Merino (70% merino, 30% camel; 120 yd [110 m]/50 g): corn yellow #3, 9 (10, 11, 12) balls.

Needles U.S. size 7 (4.5 mm): straight and 32" (80 cm) circular (cir) needles. U.S. size 8 (5 mm): straight and 32" (80 cm) circular needles. Adjust needle size if necessary to obtain the correct gauge.

Notions Stitch markers (m), stitch holders, tapestry needle, 3 mother-of-pearl buttons, ¾" (19 mm).

Gauge 17 sts and 34 rows = 4" (10 cm) in garter st on larger needles.

Stitch Guide

BOBBLE

(K1, p1, k1) in same st; turn. P3, turn. K3, turn. P3, turn. K3tog—1 st rem.

Back

With larger needles, CO 76 (84, 90, 98) sts. Work back and forth in garter st until piece measures 10½ (11, 11½, 11¾)" (26.5 [28, 29, 30] cm).

BO 7 (8, 9, 10) sts at beg of next 2 rows—62 (68, 72, 78) sts. Place rem sts on holder.

Left Front

With larger needles, CO 41 (45, 48, 52) sts. Work back and forth in garter st until piece measures 10½ (11, 11½, 11¾)" (26.5 [28, 29, 30] cm), ending with a WS row.

BO 7 (8, 9, 10) sts at beg of next RS row—34 (37, 39, 42) sts. Place rem sts on holder.

Right Front

Work right front same as left until piece measures 10½ (11, 11½, 11¾)" (26.5 [28, 29, 30] cm), ending with a RS row.

BO 7 (8, 9, 10) sts at beg of next WS row—34 (37, 39, 42) sts. Place rem sts on holder.

Sleeves

With larger needles, CO 44 (44, 46, 48) sts. Work back and forth in garter st until sleeve measures 2 (2, 2, 3¼)" (5 [5, 5, 8] cm), ending with a WS row.

NEXT ROW (INC): K1, M1, knit to last st, M1, k1—2 sts inc'd.

Rep inc row every 2¾ (2, 2, 1½)" (7 [5, 5, 4] cm) 5 (7, 7, 8) more times—56 (60, 62, 66) sts. Work even until piece measures 18 (17¾, 17¼, 17)" (46 [45, 44, 43] cm), ending with a WS row.

BO 7 (8, 9, 10) sts at beg of next 2 rows—42 (44, 44, 46) sts. Place rem sts on a holder.

Yoke

Place all the pieces onto larger cir needle as foll: front, sleeve, back, sleeve, front—214 (230, 238, 254) sts.

NEXT ROW (RS): K33 (36, 38, 41), place marker (pm), k2tog, k40 (42, 42, 44), pm, k2tog, k60 (66, 70, 76), pm, k2tog, k40 (42, 42, 44), pm, k2tog, k33 (36, 38, 41)—210 (226, 234, 250) sts.

Knit 3 (3, 3, 5) rows even.

NEXT ROW (RS, RAGLAN DEC): *Knit to 2 sts before m, k2tog, k1, ssk; rep from * 3 more times, knit to end—8 sts dec'd.

Knit 1 row even.

Rep last 2 rows 0 (0, 1, 1) more time.

NEXT ROW (RAGLAN DEC AND BUTTONHOLE): K2, BO 2 sts, *knit to 2 sts before m, k2tog, k1, ssk; rep from * 3 more times, knit to end—8 sts dec'd.

NEXT ROW: Knit to buttonhole, CO 2 sts over gap, k2.

Rep raglan dec row—186 (202, 202, 218) sts.

Knit 9 rows even and remove raglan markers.

NEXT ROW (RS): K5 (front band), pm, work Yoke Chart 11 (12, 12, 13) times, pm, k5 (front band).

Continue chart and work the second and third buttonholes where indicated on chart—98 (106, 106, 114) sts rem.

Change to smaller needles.

NEXT ROW (DEC): K2 (6, 2, 7), *k6 (4, 6, 4), k2tog; rep from * 10 (14, 11, 15) more times, knit to end—87 (91, 94, 98) sts.

Knit 3 rows even. BO all sts.

Finishing

Weave in ends. Sew sleeve and side seams. Sew underarm seams. Sew buttons to left front opposite buttonholes (buttons were sewn on with the back of the button facing).

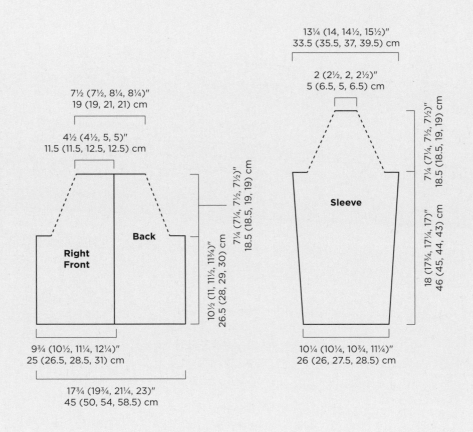

13¼ (14, 14½, 15½)"
33.5 (35.5, 37, 39.5) cm

2 (2½, 2, 2½)"
5 (6.5, 5, 6.5) cm

7½ (7½, 8¼, 8¼)"
19 (19, 21, 21) cm

4½ (4½, 5, 5)"
11.5 (11.5, 12.5, 12.5) cm

7¼ (7¼, 7½, 7½)" cm
18.5 (18.5, 19, 19) cm

7¼ (7¼, 7½, 7½)"
18.5 (18.5, 19, 19) cm

Back

Right
Front

Sleeve

10½ (11, 11½, 11¾)"
26.5 (28, 29, 30) cm

18 (17¾, 17¼, 17)"
46 (45, 44, 43) cm

9¾ (10½, 11¼, 12¼)"
25 (26.5, 28.5, 31) cm

10¼ (10¼, 10¾, 11¼)"
26 (26, 27.5, 28.5) cm

17¾ (19¾, 21¼, 23)"
45 (50, 54, 58.5) cm

Yoke Chart

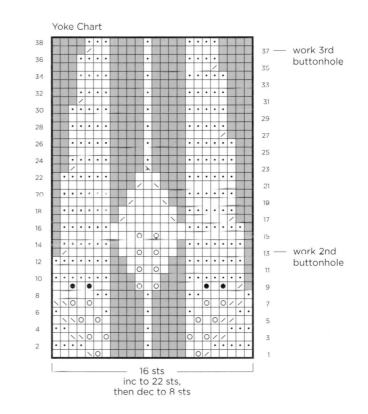

Key:

- ☐ k on RS; p on WS
- �· p on RS; k on WS
- ○ yo
- ╱ k2tog
- ╲ ssk
- ⅄ sk2p
- ● bobble (see Stitch Guide)
- ▨ no stitch
- ☐ repeat box

37 — work 3rd buttonhole

13 — work 2nd buttonhole

16 sts
inc to 22 sts,
then dec to 8 sts

Hella
More Ways than One

For the most part, these two caps are knitted from the same pattern, beginning at the top with a few stitches and worked down and out to end with a ribbed brim. Loden (pictured at left), in medium-weight yarn, has seven motifs around, and two extra rows of leaves at the end. Alfa (pictured on p. 53) is knit with a heavier yarn and has only four leaf patterns around.

		Brim Circumference	Length
LODEN CAP	in	20½	8½
	cm	52	21.5
ALFA CAP	in	19¼	8
	cm	49	20.5

Yarn Worsted weight (Medium #4). Shown in: Grignasco Loden (50% lambswool, 25% alpaca, 25% viscose; 120 yd [110 m]/50 g): lime green #754, 2 balls. Chunky (Bulky #5). Shown in: Sandnes Garn Alfa (85% pure new wool, 15% mohair; 65 yd [60 m]/50 g): gray #1042, 2 balls.

Needles

LODEN

U.S. size 8 (5 mm): 16″ (40 cm) circular (cir) and set of 4 or 5 double-pointed needles (dpn). Adjust needle size if necessary to obtain the correct gauge. U.S. size 7 (4.5 mm): 16″ (40 cm) circular.

ALFA

U.S. size 11 (8 mm): 16″ (40 cm) circular and set of 5 double-pointed needles. Adjust needle size if necessary to obtain the correct gauge.

note:

This cap is begun at the top with double-pointed needles. Change to circular needle when there are too many stitches to work on double-pointed needles.

Notions Stitch marker (m), tapestry needle.

Gauge 24 sts and 27 rnds = 4″ (10 cm) in pattern on larger needles for Loden cap; 14.5 sts and 20 rnds = 4″ (10 cm) in pattern on size 11 (8 mm) needles for Alfa cap.

Loden (see page 50)

With dpn, CO 14 sts.

ROW 1 (WS): *K1, yo, p1, yo; rep from * to last 2 sts, k1, yo, kf&b—28 sts.

Turn. Divide sts over 4 dpn and join, being careful not to twist sts. Place marker (pm) for beg of rnd.

RND 2 (RS): *K1, yo, k1, yo, k1, p1; rep from * to end—42 sts.

RND 3: *K5, p1; rep from * to end.

RND 4: *K2, yo, k1, yo, k2, p1; rep from * to end—56 sts.

RND 5: *K7, p1; rep from * to end.

RND 6: *K3, yo, k1, yo, k3, p1; rep from * to end—70 sts.

RND 7: *K9, p1; rep from * to end.

RND 8: *M1, k3, s2kp, k3, M1, p1; rep from * to end.

RND 9: Rep Rnd 7.

RND 10: *K1, M1, k2, s2kp, k2, M1, k1, p1; rep from * to end.

RND 11: *K1, p1, k5, p1, k1, p1; rep from * to end.

RND 12: *Yo, k1, yo, p1, k1, s2kp, k1, p1, yo, k1, yo, p1; rep from * to end—84 sts.

RND 13: *K3, p1; rep from * to end.

RND 14: *K1, yo, k1, yo, k1, p1, s2kp, p1, k1, yo, k1, yo, k1, p1; rep from * to end—98 sts.

RND 15: *K5, p1, k1, p1, k5, p1; rep from * to end.

RND 16: *K2, yo, k1, yo, k2, p3tog, k2, yo, k1, yo, k2, p1; rep from * to end—112 sts.

RND 17: *K7, p1; rep from * to end.

RND 18: *K3, yo, k1, yo, k3, p1; rep from * to end—140 sts.

RND 19: *K9, p1; rep from * to end.

RND 20: *K3, s2kp, k3, p1; rep from * to end—112 sts.

RND 21: Rep Rnd 17.

RND 22: *M1, k2, s2kp, k2, M1, k1; rep from * to end.

RND 23: *P1, k5, p1, k1; rep from * to end.

RND 24: *M1, p1, k1, s2kp, k1, p1, M1, k1; rep from * to end.

RND 25: K1, (p1, k3) to last 3 sts, p1, k2.

RND 26: *Yo, k1, p1, s2kp, p1, k1, yo, k1; rep from * to end.

RND 27: *K2, p1, k1, p1, k3; rep from * to end.

RND 28: *Yo, k2, p3tog, k2, yo, k1; rep from * to end.

RND 29: *K3, p1, k4; rep from * to end.

RND 30: *Yo, k3, p1, k3, yo, k1; rep from * to end—140 sts.

RND 31: *K4, p1, k5; rep from * to end.

RND 32: K4, *M1, k1, M1, k3, s2kp, k3; rep from * to last 6 sts, M1, k1, M1, k3, sl 2 as if to k2tog, knit first st of rnd, p2sso.

RND 33: *K3, p1, k1, p1, k4; rep from * to end.

RND 34: K3, *p1, M1, k1, M1, p1, k2, s2kp, k2; rep from * to last 7 sts, p1, M1, k1, M1, p1, k2, sl 2 as if to k2tog, knit first st of rnd, p2sso.

RND 35: *K2, p1, k3, p1, k3; rep from * 13 times more.

RND 36: K2, *p1, k1, yo, k1, yo, k1, p1, k1, s2kp, k1*; rep from * to last 8 sts, p1, k1, yo, k1, yo, k1, p1, k1, sl 2 as if to k2tog, knit first st of rnd, p2sso.

RND 37: *K1, p1, k5, p1, k2; rep from * to end.

RND 38: K1, *p1, k2, yo, k1, yo, k2, p1, s2kp; rep * to last 9 sts, p1, k2, yo, k1, yo, k2, p1, sl 2 as if to k2tog, knit first st of rnd, p2sso.

RND 39: *P1, k7, p1, k1; rep from * to end.

RND 40: P1, *k3, yo, k1, yo, k3, p3tog; rep from * to last 9 sts, k3, yo, k1, yo, k3, purl tog last 2 sts and first st of rnd.

RND 41: *K9, p1; rep from * to end.

RND 42: *K3, s2kp, k3, p1; rep from * to end—112 sts.

RND 43: *K7, p1; rep from * to end.

RND 44: *Yo, k2, s2kp, k2, yo, p1; rep from * to end.

RND 45: Rep Rnd 43.

RND 46: *K1, yo, k1, s2kp, k1, yo, k1, p1; rep from * to end.

RND 47: *K1, p1, k3, p1, k1, p1; rep from * to end.

RND 48: *K1, p1, s2kp, p1, k1, p1; rep from * to end—84 sts.

Change to smaller cir needle. Continue in k1, p1 rib for 2½" (6.5 cm).

Bind off in ribbing.

Weave in ends.

Alfa (at right)

With dpn, CO 8 sts.

Work Row 1, then Rnds 2–21 as for Loden Cap—64 sts.

RND 22: *Yo, k2, s2kp, k2, yo, p1; rep from * to end.

RND 23: *K7, p1; rep from * to end.

RND 24: *K1, yo, k1, s2kp, k1, yo, k1, p1; rep from * to end.

RND 25: *K1, p1, k3, p1, k1, p1; rep from * to end.

RND 26: *K1, p1, yo, s2kp, yo, p1, k1, p1; rep from * to end.

Continue in k1, p1 rib for 2½" (6.5 cm).

Bind off in ribbing.

Weave in ends.

Nikita
Blocks for a Sweater

This sweater consists of two squares. They are worked from the center out, with increases integrated with a decorative pattern that spreads out over the back and front. If you aren't wild about finishing, this sweater is for you: There are no seams to sew.

		S	M	L	XL
BUST	in	35½	38½	41¾	45
	cm	90	98	106	114.5
LENGTH	in	19	20½	22	23¾
	cm	48	52	56	60.5

Yarn DK weight (Light #3). Shown in: BC Garn Semilla (100% organic wool; 175 yd [160 m]/50 g): light turquoise ob120, 6 (6, 7, 8) balls. Laceweight (Lace #0). Shown in: BC Garn Kidmohair (70% super kidmohair, 30% polyamid; 246 yd [225 m]/25 g): light turquoise km29, 4 (5, 5, 6) balls.

Needles U.S. size 10¾ (7 mm): set of 5 double-pointed needles (dpn), 16" (40 cm) and 32" (80 cm) circular (cir). Adjust needle size if necessary to obtain the correct gauge.

Notions Stitch markers (m), stitch holders, cable needle (cn), and tapestry needle.

Gauge 14 sts and 23 rows = 4" (10 cm) in reverse St st with one strand of each yarn held together; 13 sts and 22½ rows = 4" (10 cm) in chart patt with one strand of each yarn held together.

Back

With dpn and one strand of each yarn held together, CO 12 sts. Divide sts evenly over 4 dpn—3 sts on each dpn. Join to work in the rnd, being careful not to twist sts. Place marker (pm) for beg of rnd.

Work pattern chart rows 1–38—172 sts; 43 sts in each section.

Continue cables and inc every other rnd as est 7 (10, 12, 15) more times, working sts between cables in reverse St st (purl every rnd)—228 (252, 268, 292) sts; 57 (63, 67, 73) sts in each section. Each side of square should measures about 17½ (19¼, 20¾, 22½)" (44.5 [49, 52.5, 57] cm). Pm at center of each cable.

Place sts on holders as foll: Between m1 and m2, place 57 (63, 67, 73) sts on holder for bottom rib; between m2 and m3, place first 31 (36, 38, 42) sts on holder for side seam and rem 26 (27, 29, 31) sts on holder for sleeve; between m3 and m4, place first 15 (18, 19, 22) sts on holder for shoulder, the center 27 (27, 29, 29) sts on holder for neck and rem 15 (18, 19, 22) sts on holder for rem shoulder; and between m4 and m1, place first 26 (27, 29, 31) sts on holder for sleeve and rem 31 (36, 38, 42) sts on holder for side seam.

Front

Work front same as back until there are 188 (212, 228, 252) sts; 47 (53, 57, 63) sts in each section, ending with an inc rnd. Pm at center of each cable.

Shape neck

Cut yarn and sl the first 17 (20, 21, 24) sts to right needle. Beg working back and forth across all sides.

NEXT ROW (WS): Work 175 (199, 213, 237) sts, turn leaving 13 (13, 15, 15) sts unworked for neck.

BO 3 sts at beg of next 2 rows, 2 sts at beg of next 2 rows, and 1 st at beg of next 4 rows sts. *At the same time,* continue inc before and after cables every RS row as est 5 more times—201 (225, 239, 263) sts; 57 (63, 67, 73) sts each on side and bottom edges and 15 (18, 19, 22) sts for each shoulder.

Join front and back

Return back sts to shorter cir needle as needed and hold front and back with RS tog. Join pieces using three-needle bind-off as foll: 17 (20, 21, 24) sts at shoulder, place next 26 (27, 29, 31) front sts on holder for sleeve, join next 31 (36, 38, 42) sts of front and back for side seam, place next 57 (63, 67, 73) front sts on holder for bottom rib, join next 31 (36, 38, 42) sts of front and back for side seam, place next 26 (27, 29, 31) front sts on holder for sleeve, then join rem 17 (20, 21, 24) sts at shoulder—114 (126, 134, 146) sts rem for bottom rib and 52 (54, 58, 62) sts rem for each sleeve.

Sleeves

Turn piece with WS facing. Place sts from holders at one armhole on dpn—52 (54, 58, 62) sts. Join to work in the rnd. Pm at bottom of armhole for beg of rnd.

Work in St st for 2 (2¾, 2½, 2)" (5 [7, 6, 5] cm).

NEXT RND (DEC): K2tog, knit to last 2 sts, ssk—2 sts dec'd.

Rep dec rnd every 11 (8, 8, 8) rnds 7 (8, 8, 8) more times—36 (36, 40, 44) sts rem.

Work even until sleeve measures 17 (16½, 16¼, 15¾)" (43 [42, 41, 40] cm). Continue in k2, p2 rib for 1¼" (3 cm). BO in ribbing.

Neckband

With short cir needle and RS facing, beg at left shoulder seam and pick up and k16 sts along left side of neck, k13 (13,

Chart

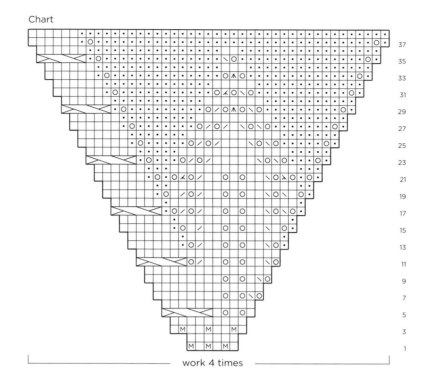

work 4 times

	k on RS; p on WS
·	p on RS; k on WS
O	yo
∕	k2tog
⋌	k3tog
＼	ssk
∧	sl 2 as if to k2tog, k1, psso
⋋	k3tog tbl
M	make 1
✕✕	3/3 LC (see Stitch Guide)

15, 15) from front holder, pick up and k16 sts along right side of neck, then k27 (27, 29, 29) from back holder—72 (72, 76, 76) sts. Join to work in the rnd. Pm for beg of rnd.

Work in k2, p2 rib for 1¼" (3 cm). BO in ribbing.

Lower Edge

Replace sts from holders at lower edge on longer cir needle—114, (126, 134, 146) sts. Join to work in the rnd. Pm for beg of rnd.

NEXT RND: K1, M1, (p2, k2) 14 (15, 16, 18) times, p2, k1, M1, (p2, k2) to end—116 (128, 136, 148) sts.

Continue in k2, p2 rib for 1¼" (3 cm). BO in ribbing

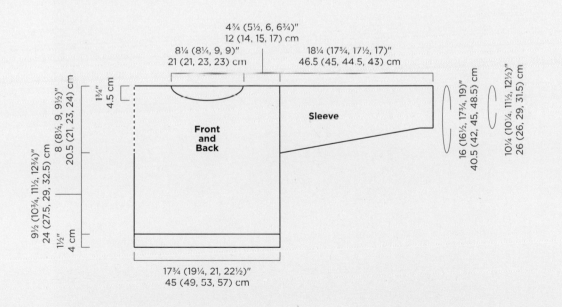

Bella
Short-Sleeve Vest with Leaf Motifs

This lovely and very feminine vest with a sumptuous leaf pattern spreads out from the neckline over a round yoke. The rest of the vest is quite simple, with ribbing edged by garter stitch bands.

		S	M	L	XL
BUST	in	33½	36¼	39	41¾
	cm	85	92	99	106
LENGTH	in	19	19¼	19¾	20½
	cm	48	49	50	52

Yarn Sportweight (#2 Fine). Shown in: Hjertegarn Alpaca Silk (60% alpaca, 30% merino wool, 10% silk; 180 yd [160 m]/50 g): dark powder 2260, 4 (5, 5, 6) balls.

Needles U.S. size 1.5 (2.5 mm): 32" (80 cm) circular (cir) needles. U.S. size 2.5 (3 mm): 32" (80 cm) circular needles. Adjust needle sizes if necessary to obtain the correct gauge.

Notions Tapestry needle, 7 mother-of-pearl buttons, ⅜–½" (10–12 mm).

Gauge 26 sts and 37 rows = 4" (10 cm) in St st on larger needles.

note:
The vest is worked from the top down. Circular needles are used to accommodate the large number of stitches.

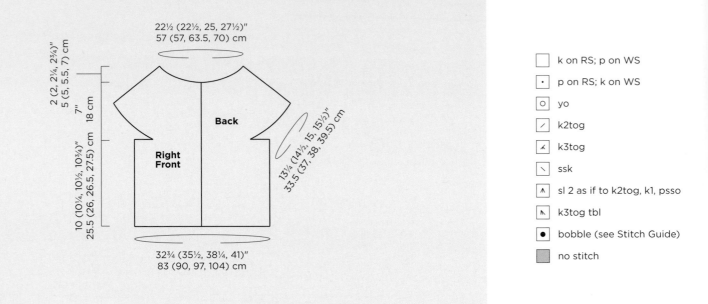

Chart legend:

- ☐ k on RS; p on WS
- · p on RS; k on WS
- ○ yo
- ╱ k2tog
- ⤣ k3tog
- ╲ ssk
- ⋀ sl 2 as if to k2tog, k1, psso
- ⤥ k3tog tbl
- ● bobble (see Stitch Guide)
- ▨ no stitch

Diagram measurements:

22½ (22½, 25, 27½)"
57 (57, 63.5, 70) cm

2 (2, 2¼, 2¾)"
5 (5, 5.5, 7) cm

7"
18 cm

Back

13¾ (14½, 15, 15½)"
33.5 (37, 38, 39.5) cm

Right Front

10 (10¼, 10½, 10¾)"
25.5 (26, 26.5, 27.5) cm

32¾ (35½, 38¼, 41)"
83 (90, 97, 104) cm

Yoke

With smaller cir needle, CO 147 (147, 153, 159) sts. Work back and forth, knit 5 rows and inc 0 (0, 10, 20) sts evenly spaced across last row—147 (147, 163, 179) sts.

Change to larger cir needle.

NEXT ROW (WS): K1 (edge st), p1, *k7, p1; rep from * to last st, k1 (edge st).

NEXT ROW: K1 (edge st), work first 16 sts of Yoke Chart, work next 16 sts of chart 8 (8, 9, 10) times, k1 (edge st).

Continue in chart patt through row 64—327 (327, 363, 399) sts.

Divide work

NEXT ROW (RS): Work 46 (46, 52, 58) sts for left front, BO next 70 (70, 76, 82) sts in patt for sleeve, work 95 (95, 107, 119) sts for back, BO next 70 (70, 76, 82) sts in patt for sleeve, work rem 46 (46, 52, 58) sts for right front—187 (187, 211, 235) sts.

NEXT ROW: Continue in rib as established, *work to armhole, CO 16 (25, 22, 19) sts over gap for underarm; rep from * once more, then work to end—219 (237, 255, 273) sts. *Note:* If you want a wider bust circumference (especially for sizes L and XL), you can, for example, CO 4 sts more at

both sides between back and front and work the extra sts in reverse St st.

Continue in rib patt until piece measures 17 (17¼, 17½, 17¾)" (43 [44, 44.5, 45] cm) from beg along center back. BO all sts in rib.

Finishing

Weave in ends. Block to finished measurements.

Buttonband

With smaller cir needle and RS facing, pick up and k126 (130, 133, 136) sts along left edge. Knit 7 rows. BO kwise.

Buttonhole band

With smaller cir needle and RS facing, pick up and k126 (130, 133, 136) sts along right edge. Knit 2 rows.

NEXT ROW (WS, BUTTONHOLE): K2 (4, 2, 4), *BO 2 for buttonhole, k18 (18, 19, 19); rep from * 5 more times, BO 2 for buttonhole, knit to end.

NEXT ROW: CO 2 sts over each buttonhole gap.

Knit 3 more rows. BO kwise.

Sew buttons to buttonband opposite buttons.

Yoke Chart

work 8 (8, 9, 10) times

Structure Patterns

Structure patterns are usually knit and purl combinations, but I've broadened the definition to include smocking and patterns combining lace, twist, and rib stitches—or any pattern motif that provides an abundance of structure.

Gerda
A Feminine Guernsey

This long sweater is a feminine variation of the classic English Guernsey with knit and purl motifs. The sweater goes equally well with jeans and rubber boots or a skirt and heels. The patterns really pop in the natural color tweedy yarn and are quite easy to knit.

		S	M	L	XL
BUST	in	37¾	40	42	44¼
	cm	96	101.5	106.5	112.5
LENGTH	in	31½	32	32¼	32¾
	cm	80	81	82	83

Yarn Chunky weight (Bulky #5). Shown in: Sandnes Garn Fritidsgarn (100% pure new wool; 77 yd [70 m]/50 g): natural white #2641, 14 (15, 16, 17) balls.

Needles U.S. size 9 (5.5 mm) straight. U.S. size 10 (6 mm): straight. Adjust needle sizes if necessary to obtain the correct gauge. U.S. size 8 (5 mm): 32" (80 cm) circular (cir).

Notions Stitch marker; Six 1" [25 mm] leather buttons.

Gauge 15 sts and 21 rows = 4" (10 cm) in pattern on U.S. size 10 (6 mm) needles.

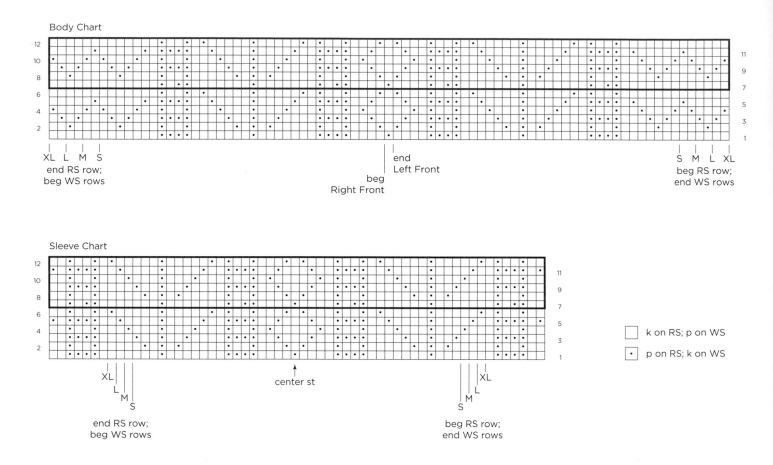

Body Chart

XL L M S
end RS row;
beg WS rows

end
Left Front

beg
Right Front

S M L XL
beg RS row;
end WS rows

Sleeve Chart

XL
L
M
S
end RS row;
beg WS rows

center st

XL
M
S
beg RS row;
end WS rows

☐ k on RS; p on WS

· p on RS; k on WS

Back

With U.S. size 9 (5.5 mm) needles, CO 78 (82, 86, 90) sts.

ROW 1 (WS): K1 (edge st), p1, k2, *p2, k2; rep from * to last 2 sts, p1, k1 (edge st).

ROW 2: K1 (edge st), k1, p2, *k2, p2; rep from * to last 2 sts, k1, k1 (edge st).

Rep Rows 1 and 2 until ribbing measures about 2¾" (7 cm), ending with a RS row.

NEXT (DEC) ROW (WS): Work 2 (4, 6, 8) sts as established, (p2tog, work 10 sts) 6 times, p2tog, work to end—71 (75, 79, 83) sts.

Change to U.S. size 10 (6 mm) needles.

ROW 1 (RS): K1 (edge st), work Row 1 of Body Chart, k1 (edge st).

Keep edge sts in garter st, work even until piece measures 9¾" (25 cm), ending with a WS row.

NEXT (DEC) ROW (RS): K1 (edge st), k2tog, work in established patt to last 3 sts, ssk, k1 (edge st)—2 sts dec'd.

Rep dec row every 14 rows twice more—65 (69, 73, 77) sts. Work even until piece measures 18½ (19, 19¼, 19¾)" (47 [48, 49, 50] cm), ending with a WS row.

NEXT (INC) ROW (RS): K1 (edge st), M1, work in established patt to last st, M1, k1 (edge st)—2 sts inc'd.

Rep inc row every 8 rows twice more—71 (75, 79, 83) sts. Work even until piece measures 23½" (60 cm).

Shape armholes

BO 4 (5, 5, 6) sts at the beg of next 2 rows. Dec 1 st each end of every RS row 3 times—57 (59, 63, 65) sts rem. Work even until armhole measures 7 (7½, 7¾, 8¼)" (18 [19, 20, 21] cm), ending with a WS row.

Shape neck and shoulders

NEXT ROW (RS): BO 5 (6, 6, 6) sts, work next 12 (12, 13, 14) sts in established patt, place next 23 (23, 25, 25) sts on holder for back neck, join a second ball of yarn and work rem 17 (18, 19, 20) sts. Work each side separately.

NEXT ROW: BO 5 (6, 6, 6) sts, work to end—12 (12, 13, 14) sts rem each side.

BO 6 sts at beg of next 4 (4, 2, 0) rows, then 7 sts at beg of next 0 (0, 2, 4) rows.

Left Front

With U.S. size 9 (5.5 mm) needles, CO 39 (43, 43, 47) sts and work in ribbing.

ROW 1 (WS): K1 (edge st), *p2, k2; rep from * to last 2 sts, p1, k1 (edge st).

ROW 2: K1 (edge st), k1, *p2, k2; rep from * to last st, k1 (edge st).

Rep Rows 1 and 2 until ribbing measures about 2¾" (7 cm), ending with a RS row.

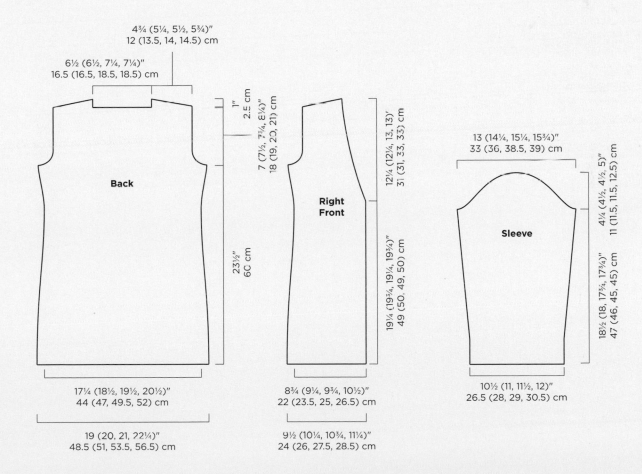

Back

4¾ (5¼, 5½, 5¾)"
12 (13.5, 14, 14.5) cm

6½ (6½, 7¼, 7¼)"
16.5 (16.5, 18.5, 18.5) cm

1"
2.5 cm

7 (7½, 7¾, 8¼)"
18 (19, 20, 21) cm

23½"
60 cm

17¼ (18½, 19½, 20½)"
44 (47, 49.5, 52) cm

19 (20, 21, 22¼)"
48.5 (51, 53.5, 56.5) cm

Right Front

12¼ (12¼, 13, 13)"
31 (31, 33, 33) cm

19¼ (19¾, 19¼, 19¾)"
49 (50, 49, 50) cm

8¾ (9¼, 9¾, 10½)"
22 (23.5, 25, 26.5) cm

9½ (10¼, 10¾, 11¼)"
24 (26, 27.5, 28.5) cm

Sleeve

13 (14¼, 15¼, 15¾)"
33 (36, 38.5, 39) cm

4¼ (4½, 4½, 5)"
11 (11.5, 11.5, 12.5) cm

18½ (18, 17¾, 17¾)"
47 (46, 45, 45) cm

10½ (11, 11½, 12)"
26.5 (28, 29, 30.5) cm

NEXT (DEC) ROW (WS): Work 6 (6, 10, 6) sts as established, (p2tog, work 10 [6, 10, 6] sts) 2 (4, 2, 4) times, p2tog, work to end—36 (38, 40, 42) sts.

Change to U.S. size 10 (6 mm) needles.

ROW 1 (RS): K1 (edge st), work Row 1 of Body Chart, k1 (edge st).

Keep edge sts in garter st, work even until piece measures 9¾" (25 cm), ending with a WS row.

NEXT (DEC) ROW (RS): K1 (edge st), k2tog, work in established patt to end—1 st dec'd.

Rep dec row every 14 rows twice more—33 (35, 37, 39) sts. Work even until piece measures 18½ (19, 19¼, 19¾)" (47 [48, 49, 50] cm), ending with a WS row.

NEXT (INC) ROW (RS): K1 (edge st), M1, work in established patt to end—1 st inc'd.

Rep inc row every 8 rows twice more, and *at the same time,* when piece measures 19¼ (19¾, 19¼, 19¾)" (49 [50, 49, 50] cm), end with a WS row.

Shape neck

NEXT (NECK DEC) ROW (RS): Work to last 3 sts, ssk, k1—1 st dec'd. Cont side shaping as established, rep neck dec row (every 4 rows, then every 6 rows) 5 (5, 6, 6) times, then every 6 rows 1 (1, 0, 0) more time. *At the same time,* when piece measures 23½" (60 cm), end with a WS row.

Shape armhole

BO 4 (5, 5, 6) sts at beg of next RS row. Dec 1 st at armhole edge every RS row 3 times—17 (18, 19, 20) sts rem when all shaping is complete.

Work even until armhole measures 7 (7½, 7¾, 8¼)" (18 [19, 20, 21] cm), ending with a WS row.

Shape shoulder

BO 5 sts at beg of next 1 (0, 0, 0) RS rows, 6 sts at beg of next 2 (3, 2, 1) RS row(s), then 7 sts at beg of next 0 (0, 0, 1) RS row.

Right Front

With U.S. size 9 (5.5 mm) needles, CO 39 (43, 43, 47) sts and work in ribbing.

ROW 1 (WS): K1 (edge st), p1, *k2, p2; rep from * to last st, k1 (edge st).

ROW 2: K1 (edge st), *k2, p2; rep from * to last 2 sts, k1, k1 (edge st).

Rep Rows 1 and 2 until ribbing measures about 2¾" (7 cm), ending with a RS row.

NEXT (DEC) ROW (WS): Work 6 (6, 10, 6) sts as established, (p2tog, work 10 [6, 10, 6] sts) 2 (4, 2, 4) times, p2tog, work to end—36 (38, 40, 42) sts.

Change to U.S. size 10 (6 mm) needles.

ROW 1 (RS): K1 (edge st), work Row 1 of Body Chart, k1 (edge st).

Keep edge sts in garter st, work even until piece measures 9¾" (25 cm), ending with a WS row.

NEXT (DEC) ROW (RS): K1 (edge st), work in established patt to last 3 sts, ssk, k1—1 st dec'd.

Rep dec row every 14 rows twice more—33 (35, 37, 39) sts. Work even until piece measures 18½ (19, 19¼, 19¾)" (47 [48, 49, 50] cm), ending with a WS row.

NEXT (INC) ROW (RS): K1 (edge st), work in established patt to last st, M1, k1—1 st inc'd.

Rep inc row every 8 rows twice more, and *at the same time,* when piece measures 19¼ (19¾, 19¼, 19¾)" (49 [50, 49, 50] cm), end with a WS row.

Shape neck

NEXT (NECK DEC) ROW (RS): K1, k2tog, work to end—1 st dec'd. Cont side shaping as established, rep neck dec row (every 4 rows, then every 6 rows) 5 (5, 6, 6) times, then every 6 rows 1 (1, 0, 0) more time. *At the same time,* when piece measures 23½" (60 cm), end with a RS row.

Shape armhole

BO 4 (5, 5, 6) sts at beg of next WS row. Dec 1 st at armhole edge every RS row 3 times—17 (18, 19, 20) sts rem when all shaping is complete.

Work even until armhole measures 7 (7½, 7¾, 8¼)" (18 [19, 20, 21] cm), ending with a RS row.

Shape shoulder

BO 5 sts at beg of next 1 (0, 0, 0) WS rows, 6 sts at beg of next 2 (3, 2, 1) WS row(s), then 7 sts at beg of next 0 (0, 0, 1) WS row.

Sleeves

With U.S. size 9 (5.5 mm) needles, CO 50 (50, 54, 54) sts.

ROW 1 (WS): K1 (edge st), p1, k2, *p2, k2; rep from * to last 2 sts, p1, k1 (edge st).

ROW 2: K1 (edge st), k1, p2, *k2, p2; rep from * to last 2 sts, k1, k1 (edge st).

Rep Rows 1 and 2 until ribbing measures about 2¾" (7 cm), ending with a RS row.

NEXT (DEC) ROW (WS): Dec 11 (9, 11, 9) sts evenly spaced over purl sts only—39 (41, 43, 45) sts.

Change to U.S. size 10 (6 mm) needles.

ROW 1 (RS): K1 (edge st), work Row 1 of Sleeve Chart, k1 (edge st).

Keep edge sts in garter st, work 13 (11, 9, 9) rows even, ending with a WS row.

NEXT (INC) ROW (RS): K1 (edge st), M1, work in established patt to last st, M1, k1 (edge st) —2 sts inc'd.

Rep inc row every 14 (12, 10, 10) rows 4 (5, 6, 6) more times and work new sts into patt—49 (53, 57, 59) sts. Work even until piece measures 18½ (18, 17¾, 17¾)" (47 [46, 45, 45] cm), ending with a WS row.

Shape cap

BO 3 sts at beg of next 2 (2, 4, 4) rows, 2 sts at beg of next 4 (4, 2, 2) rows. Dec 1 st each end every RS row 5 (6, 6, 7) times. BO 2 sts at beg of next 2 rows, 3 sts at beg of next 2 rows, then 4 sts at beg of next 2 rows—7 (9, 11, 11) sts. BO rem sts.

Finishing

Weave in ends. Block pieces to finished measurements.

Sew shoulder seams.

Front band

With cir needle and RS facing, beg at bottom of right front edge, pick up and k81 (83, 81, 83) sts along right front to beg of neck shaping, place marker, pick up and k50 (50, 53, 53) sts along shaped edge to shoulder 32 (32, 34, 34) along back neck, 50 (50, 53, 53) sts along shaped edge of left front edge to beg of neck shaping, then 81 (83, 81, 83) sts along left front to lower edge—294 (298, 302, 306) sts.

ROW 1 (WS): P2, *k2, p2; rep from * to end.

ROW 2: *K2, p2; rep from * to last 2 sts, k2.

NEXT (BUTTONHOLE) ROW: Work in established rib to marker, *BO 3 sts for buttonhole (1 st on right needle after gap), work 11 sts; rep from * 4 more times, BO 3 sts for buttonhole, work to end.

NEXT ROW: CO 3 sts over gap for each buttonhole.

Work 3 rows even. BO in ribbing.

Sew sleeve and side seams. Sew in sleeves. Sew buttons to left band opposite buttonholes.

Raya
Feminine Hoodie

You'll need to pay close attention while you work on this sweater. The wide pattern band has ribbing, lace, and twisted stitches that run up the front and around the hood. The hooded sweater ends smoothly at the waist because of the wide ribbed band and it goes equally well with skirts or pants.

		S	M	L	XL
BUST	in	33½	36½	39¼	43
	cm	85	93	100	109
LENGTH	in	22½	22¾	23½	24½
	cm	57	58	59.5	62

notes:

When ending the right front, mark the last chart row worked. End the left front by working one more or one fewer row so that both halves will be ready to begin the hood on the same number row on both charts, making it easier to follow both charts.

Yarn DK weight (Light #3). Shown in: Rowan Felted Tweed DK (50% merino wool, 25% alpaca, 25% viscose; 191 yd [175 m]/50 g): seasalter #178, 7 (7, 8, 9) balls.

Needles U.S. size 4 (3.5 mm): straight. U.S. size 6 (4 mm): straight. Adjust needle sizes if necessary to obtain the correct gauge. Spare needle in U.S. size 6 (4 mm) for three-needle bind-off.

Notions 2 cable needles (cn), stitch holders, and tapestry needle.

Gauge 22 sts and 32 rows = 4" (10 cm) in St st on larger needles; 38 sts = 5" (12.5 cm) wide in Left and Right Front chart.

Back

With smaller needles, CO 95 (104, 113, 122) sts.

ROW 1 (WS): K1 (edge st), k1, (p1, k2) to last 3 sts, p1, k1, k1 (edge st).

ROW 2: K1 (edge st), p1 (k1, p2) to last 3 sts, k1, p1, k1 (edge st).

Rep Rows 1 and 2 until rib measures 4¼ (4¾, 5¼, 5¼)" (11 [12, 13, 13] cm), ending with a WS row and inc 1 (0, dec 1, 0) st on last row—96 (104, 112, 122) sts.

Change to larger needles.

Continue in reverse St st until piece measures 14¾ (14½, 14¾, 15½)" (37.5 [37, 37.5, 39.5] cm), ending with a WS row.

Shape armholes

BO 4 sts at beg of next 2 rows and 2 sts at beg of next 2 (2, 4, 6) rows. Dec 1 st each end every RS row 2 (3, 2, 2) times—80 (86, 92, 98) sts rem.

Work even until armhole measures 7 (7½, 7¾, 8¼)" (18 [19, 20, 21] cm), ending with a WS row.

Shape shoulders

BO 5 (6, 6, 7) sts at beg of next 6 (6, 2, 2) rows, 7 sts at beg of next 0 (0, 4, 0) rows, then 8 sts at beg of next 0 (0, 0, 4) rows—50 (50, 52, 52) sts rem. Place rem sts on holder for hood.

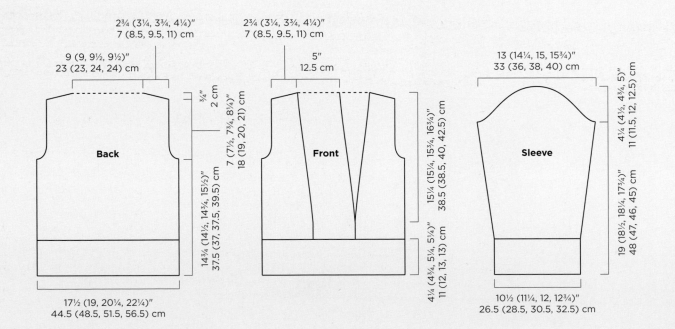

Front

Work rib same as for back—96 (104, 112, 122).

Change to larger needles.

NEXT ROW (RS): P29 (33, 37, 42), work Row 1 of Right Front chart over next 38 sts, p29 (33, 37, 42).

NEXT ROW: K29 (33, 37, 42), work Row 2 of Right Front chart over next 38 sts, place rem 29 (33, 37, 42) sts on holder for left front—67 (71, 75, 80) sts rem for right front.

Right Front

Continue in reverse St st and patt as established until piece measures 6¼ (7½, 7¾, 7¾)" (16 [19, 20, 20] cm), ending with a RS row.

Shape neck

NEXT (DEC) ROW (WS): Knit to 2 sts before patt, ssk, work in patt to end—1 st dec'd.

Rep dec row every 18 (18, 16, 18) rows 5 (5, 6, 6) more times. *At the same time,* when piece measures 13¾ (14½, 15, 15½)" (35 [37, 38, 39.5] cm), ending with a RS row.

Shape armhole

BO 4 sts at beg of next WS row, 2 sts at beg of next 1 (1, 2, 3) WS row(s). Dec 1 st at beg of WS rows 2 (3, 2, 2) times—53 (56, 58, 61) sts rem when all shaping is complete. Work even until armhole measures 7 (7½, 7¾, 8¼)" (18 [19, 20, 21] cm), end with a RS row.

Shape shoulder

BO at beg of WS rows 5 sts 3 (0, 0, 0) times, 6 sts 0 (3, 1, 0) time(s), 7 sts 0 (0, 2, 1) time(s), then 8 sts 0 (0, 0, 2) times. Place rem 38 sts (lace/cable pattern) on a holder for hood.

Left Front

Place 29 (33, 37, 42) sts on hold for left front on smaller needle ready to work a WS row. With larger needles, CO 38 sts.

NEXT ROW (WS): Work Row 2 of Left Front chart across CO sts, knit 29 (33, 37, 42) sts from smaller needle—67 (71, 75, 80) sts.

Continue in reverse St st and patt as established until piece measures 6¼ (7½, 7¾, 7¾)" (16 [19, 20, 20] cm), ending with a RS row.

Shape neck

NEXT (DEC) ROW (WS): Work in patt over first 38 sts, k2tog, knit to end—1 st dec'd.

Rep dec row every 18 (18, 16, 18) rows 5 (5, 6, 6) more times. *At the same time,* when piece measures 13¾ (14½, 15, 15½)" (35 [37, 38, 39.5] cm), ending with a WS row.

Shape armhole

BO 4 sts at beg of next RS row, 2 sts at beg of next 1 (1, 2, 3) RS row(s). Dec 1 st at beg of RS rows 2 (3, 2, 2) times—53 (56, 58, 61) sts rem when all shaping is complete. Work even until armhole measures 7 (7½, 7¾, 8¼)" (18 [19, 20, 21] cm), ending with a WS row.

Shape shoulder

BO at beg of RS rows 5 sts 3 (0, 0, 0) times, 6 sts 0 (3, 1, 0) time(s), 7 sts 0 (0, 2, 1) time(s), then 8 sts 0 (0, 0, 2) times. Place rem 38 sts (lace/cable pattern) on a holder for hood.

Sleeves

With smaller needles, CO 56 (59, 62, 68) sts.

Work rib same as for back and inc 2 (3, 4, 2) sts evenly spaced across last row—58 (62, 66, 70) sts.

Change to larger needles. Continue even in reverse St st until sleeve measures 7¾ (6¼, 6¼, 6¼)" (20 [16, 16, 16] cm), ending with a RS row.

NEXT (INC) ROW (WS): K1, M1, knit to last st, M1, k1—2 sts inc'd.

Rep inc row every 12 rows 6 (7, 7, 7) more times—72 (78, 82, 86) sts. Work even until piece measures 19 (18½, 18, 17¾)" (48 [47, 46, 45] cm), ending with a WS row.

Shape cap

BO 4 sts at beg of next 2 rows, 2 sts at beg of next 6 rows. Dec 1 st at each of every other row 7 times. BO 2 sts at beg of next 6 (8, 10, 12) rows, then 3 sts at beg of next 6 rows—8 (10, 10, 10) sts rem. BO rem sts.

Finishing

Weave in ends. Block pieces to finished measurements. Sew shoulder seams.

Hood

Place sts from holders at fronts and back onto larger needles—126 (126, 128, 128) sts.

Continue even in patt at both ends and work rem sts in reverse St st until hood measures 11¾ (11¾, 12¼, 12¼)" (30 [30, 31, 31] cm) along center of back.

Divide sts evenly with 63 (63, 64, 64) sts on each of 2 needles. Hold needles with RS together. Join using three-needle bind-off.

Sew sts cast-on to beg left front to WS behind right front.

Right Front chart

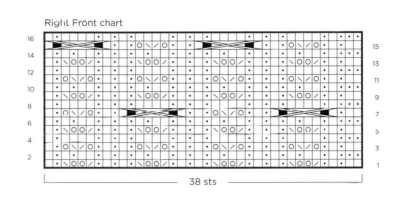

38 sts

Left Front chart

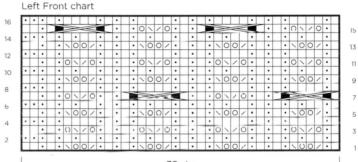

38 sts

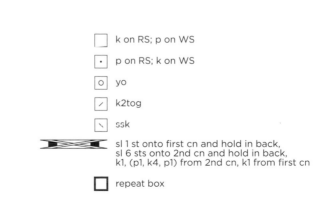

☐ k on RS; p on WS

· p on RS; k on WS

◯ yo

╱ k2tog

╲ ssk

sl 1 st onto first cn and hold in back,
sl 6 sts onto 2nd cn and hold in back,
k1, (p1, k4, p1) from 2nd cn, k1 from first cn

☐ repeat box

Smilla
Sweet and Nostalgic

An ultrafeminine color and fine shaping distinguish this lovely sweater. The rounded yoke is worked in a smock pattern with the decreases integrated into the pattern that becomes closer and closer as it is worked to the top of the yoke.

		S	M	L	XL
BUST	in	33½	36¼	39¾	42½
	cm	85	92	101	108
LENGTH	in	20½	20½	20¾	21¼
	cm	52	52	53	54

Yarn DK weight (Light #3). Shown in: Sandnes Garn Alpaca (100% baby alpaca; 120 yd [110 m]/50 g): #4812 light powder, 7 (8, 9, 9) balls.

Needles U.S. size 2.5 (3 mm): straight and 24" (60 cm) circular (cir). U.S. size 4 (3.5 mm): straight and 32" (80 cm) cir. Adjust needle sizes if necessary to obtain the correct gauge.

Notions Stitch holders, tapestry needle, seven ⅝" (15 mm) mother-of-pearl buttons.

Gauge 22 sts and 32 rows = 4" (10 cm) in St st on larger needles.

Stitch Guide

SMOCK A

Insert right needle between the 6th and 7th sts on left needle, yarn over and draw through the loop, leaving stitches on left needle, p2tog, p3, k1.

SMOCK B

Insert right needle between the 6th and 7th sts on left needle, yarn over and draw through the loop, leaving stitches on left needle, p2tog, p1, p2tog, k1—1 stitch decreased.

SMOCK C

Insert right needle between the 5th and 6th sts on left needle, yarn over and draw through the loop, leaving stitches on left needle, p2tog, p2, k1.

SMOCK D

Insert right needle between the 5th and 6th sts on left needle, yarn over and draw through the loop, leaving stitches on left needle, (p2tog) twice, k1—1 st decreased.

SMOCK E

Insert right needle between the 4th and 5th sts on left needle, yarn over and draw through the loop, leaving stitches on left needle, p2tog, p1, k1.

Back

With smaller needles, CO 96 (102, 112, 120) sts. Knit 7 rows.

Change to larger needles. Continue in reverse St st and keep first st and last st of every row in garter st for edge sts. Work until piece measures 2" (5 cm), ending with a RS row.

NEXT (DEC) ROW (WS): K1, k2tog, knit to last 3 sts, ssk, k1—2 sts dec'd.

Rep dec row every 12 rows 3 more times—88 (94, 104, 112) sts.

Work even until piece measures 8½" (21.5 cm), ending with a RS row.

NEXT (INC) ROW (WS): K1, M1, knit to last st, M1, k1—2 sts inc'd.

Rep inc row every 8 rows 3 more times—96 (102, 112, 120) sts. Work even until piece measures 13" (33 cm), ending with a WS row.

Shape armholes

BO 9 (10, 10, 11) sts at beg of next 2 rows—78 (82, 92, 98) sts.

Work 1 row even.

NEXT (DEC) ROW (WS): K1, k2tog, knit to last 3 sts, ssk, k1—2 sts dec'd.

Rep dec row every WS row 3 (3, 4, 5) more times—70 (74, 82, 86) sts. Place rem sts on holder.

Left Front

With smaller needles, CO 47 (51, 56, 60) sts. Knit 7 rows.

Change to larger needles. Continue in reverse St st and keep first st and last st of every row in garter st for edge sts. Work until piece measures 2" (5 cm), ending with a RS row.

NEXT (DEC) ROW (WS): Knit to last 3 sts, ssk, k1—1 st dec'd.

Rep dec row every 12 rows 3 more times—43 (47, 52, 56) sts. *At the same time,* when piece is 8 rows shorter than back to armhole, end with a WS row.

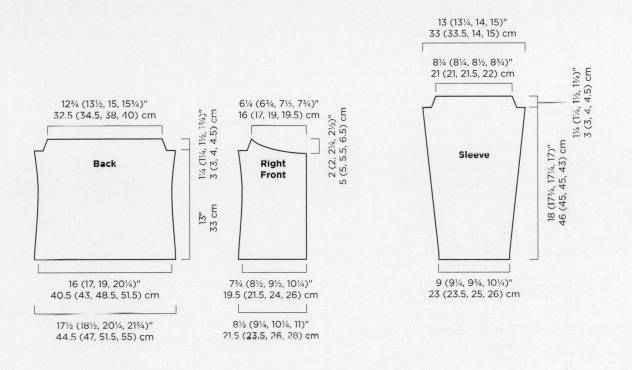

Shape neck

SHORT-ROW (RS): Purl to 3 sts before end of row, w&t.

Rep short-row every RS row 7 (7, 8, 9) more times, working w&t 3 sts before turn on previous RS row. *At the same time,* when piece measures 13" (33 cm), end with a WS row.

Shape armhole

BO 9 (10, 10, 11) sts at beg of next RS row—38 (41, 46, 49) sts.

NEXT (DEC) ROW (WS): Knit to last 3 sts, ssk, k1—1 st dec'd.

Rep dec row every WS row 3 (3, 4, 5) more times—34 (37, 41, 43) sts.

NEXT ROW (RS): Purl across all sts, hiding wraps by working them tog with the wrapped sts when you com to them. Place rem sts on holder.

Right Front

Work same as left front until piece measures 2" (5 cm), ending with a RS row.

NEXT (DEC) ROW (WS): K1, k2tog, knit to end—1 st dec'd.

Rep dec row every 12 rows 3 more times—43 (47, 52, 56) sts. *At the same time,* when piece is 8 rows shorter than back to armhole, end with a RS row.

Shape neck

SHORT-ROW (WS): Knit to 3 sts before end of row, w&t.

Rep short-row every WS row 7 (7, 8, 9) more times, working next w&t 3 sts before turn on previous RS row. *At the same time,* when piece measures 13" (33 cm), end with a RS row.

Shape armhole

BO 9 (10, 10, 11) sts at beg of next WS row—38 (41, 46, 49) sts.

NEXT (DEC) ROW (WS): K1, k2tog, knit to next short-row turn—1 st dec'd.

Rep dec row every WS row 3 (3, 4, 5) more times—34 (37, 41, 43) sts.

NEXT ROW (WS): Knit across all sts, hiding wraps by working them tog with the wrapped sts when you come to them. Place rem sts on holder.

Sleeves

With smaller needles, CO 49 (51, 53, 56) sts. Work 7 rows in k1, p1 rib.

Change to larger needles. Continue in reverse St st and keep first st and last st of every row in garter st for edge sts. Work until piece measures about 3½ (3, 4¼, 3)" (9 [7.5, 11, 7.5] cm), ending with a WS row.

NEXT (INC) ROW (RS): K1, M1p, purl to last st, M1p, k1—2 sts inc'd.

Rep inc row every 10 (10, 8, 8) rows 10 (10, 11, 12) times more—71 (73, 77, 82) sts. Work even until piece measures 18 (17¾, 17¼, 17)" (46 [45, 44, 43] cm).

Shape cap

BO 9 (10, 10, 11) sts at beg of next 2 rows—53 (53, 57, 60) sts.

Work 1 row even.

NEXT (DEC) ROW (WS): K1, k2tog, knit to last 3 sts, ssk, k1—2 sts dec'd.

Rep dec row every WS row 3 (3, 4, 5) more times—45 (45, 47, 48) sts. Place rem sts on holder.

Yoke

With RS facing, place all pieces on larger cir needle as foll: right front, sleeve, back, sleeve, then left front—228 (238, 258, 268) sts. Join yarn to beg with a RS row.

ROW 1 (RS): K1 (edge st), Smock A, (p4, Smock A) 22 (23, 25, 26) times, k1 (edge st).

ROW 2: K1 (edge st), p1, *k4, p1; rep from * to last st, k1 (edge st).

ROWS 3-6: Work in rib as established.

ROW 7: K1 (edge st), k1, (p4, Smock A) 22 (23, 25, 26) times, p4, k1, k1 (edge st).

ROW 8: K1 (edge st), p1, *k4, p1; rep from * to last st, k1 (edge st).

ROWS 9-12: Work in rib as established.

ROW 13: K1 (edge st), Smock B, (p4, Smock B) 22 (23, 25, 26) times, k1 (edge st)—205 (214, 232, 241) sts.

ROW 14: K1 (edge st), p1, *k3, p1, k4, p1; rep from * to last 5 sts, k3, p1, k1 (edge st).

ROWS 15–18: Work even in rib as established.

ROW 19: K1 (edge st), k1, (p3, Smock B) 22 (23, 25, 26) times, p3, k1, k1 (edge st)—183 (191, 207, 215) sts.

ROW 20: K1 (edge st), p1, *k3, p1; rep from * to last st, k1 (edge st).

ROWS 21–24: Work even in rib as established.

ROW 25: K1 (edge st), Smock C, (p3, Smock C) 22 (23, 25, 26) times, k1 (edge st).

ROW 26: K1 (edge st), p1, *k3, p1; rep from * to last st, k1 (edge st).

ROWS 27–30: Work in rib as established.

ROW 31: K1 (edge st), k1, (p3, Smock D) 22 (23, 25, 26) times, p3, k1, k1 (edge st)—161 (168, 182, 189) sts.

ROW 32: K1 (edge st), p1, *k3, p1, k2, p1; rep from * to last 5 sts, k3, p1, k1 (edge st).

ROWS 33–36: Work even in rib as established.

ROW 37: K1 (edge st), Smock D, (p2, Smock D) 22 (23, 25, 26) times, k1 (edge st)—138 (144, 156, 162) sts.

ROW 38: K1 (edge st), p1, *k2, p1; rep from * to last st, k1 (edge st).

ROWS 39–40: Work even in rib as established.

ROW 41: K1 (edge st), k1, p2, (Smock E, p2) 22 (23, 25, 26) times, k1 (edge st).

ROW 42: K1, p1, *k2, p1; rep from * to last st, k1 (edge st).

Without working, sl first 2 sts to right needle, pass edge st over 2nd st and off needle; rep at opposite end of needle—136 (142, 154, 160) sts. Place rem sts on holder.

Finishing

Weave in ends. Block pieces to finished measurements.

Sew sleeve and side seams. Seam underarm seams.

Buttonband

With smaller needles and RS facing, beg at neck edge, pick up and k103 (103, 105, 107) sts along left front to bottom edge.

Work in k1, p1 rib for 5 rows. BO in ribbing.

Buttonhole band

With smaller needles and RS facing, beg at bottom edge, pick up and k103 (103, 105, 107) sts along right front to neck.

Work in k1, p1 rib for 1 row.

NEXT (BUTTONHOLE) ROW (RS): Work 13 (13, 15, 12) sts, *BO 2 for buttonhole (1 st on RH needle after gap, work 14 (14, 14, 15) more sts; rep from * 4 times more, BO 2 for buttonhole, work to end.

NEXT ROW: CO 2 sts over gap for each buttonhole.

Work in rib for 2 more rows. BO in ribbing.

Neckband

Place neck sts on smaller needles. With RS facing, pick up and k4 along end of buttonhole band,

Work in k1, p1 rib across neck sts and dec 15 (17, 23, 25) sts evenly spaced across these st, pick up and k4 along end of buttonband—131 (135, 141, 145) sts.

Work in k1, p1 rib for 1 row.

NEXT (BUTTONHOLE) ROW (RS): Work 2 sts, BO 2 for buttonhole, work to end.

NEXT ROW: CO 2 sts over gap for buttonhole.

Work in rib for 2 more rows. BO in ribbing.

Sew buttons to buttonband opposite buttonholes.

Paula
Reversible Poncho

This poncho is knit from the top down and ends just below the elbow. If you want a larger, more covering garment, you just have to work another repeat of the lace design. The pattern is pretty on both sides, so, if you weave in the ends invisibly, you'll have two ponchos with the knitting of one.

		S / M	L / XL
BOTTOM CIRCUMFERENCE	in	52	56
	cm	132	142
LENGTH ALONG CENTER	in	19¾	19¾
	cm	50	50

notes:

The poncho is worked from the top down using 3 strands of yarn held together throughout: 2 strands Highland and 1 strand Alpaca 1.

If you add an extra pattern repeat in length, you'll need one more ball of Highland.

Yarn Fingering weight (Superfine #1). Shown in: Isager Highland (100% lambswool; 306 yd [280 m]/50 g): thistle, 4 (4) balls. Laceweight (Superfine #1). Shown in: Isager Alpaca 1 (100% alpaca; 875 yd [800 m]/100 g): natural gray #2105, 1 (1) ball.

Needles U.S. size 8 (5 mm): 16" (40 cm) circular (cir). U.S. size 10 (6 mm): 24" (60 cm) and 32" (80 cm) circular. Adjust needle size if necessary to obtain the correct gauge.

Notions Stitch marker, tapestry needle.

Gauge 15 sts and 24 rows = 4" (10 cm) in St st on larger needles.

Poncho

With smaller cir needle, CO 78 (84) sts. Join, being careful not to twist sts. Place marker (pm) for beg of rnd.

RND 1: *P1, k5; rep from * around.

Rep Rnd 1 until piece measures 4" (10 cm).

Change to larger cir needle. Work even in rib for 2 rnds.

NEXT (INC) RND: *P1, M1, k5; rep from * around—91 (98) sts.

Work 1 rnd even in p1, k6 rib.

NEXT (INC) RND: *P1, k6, M1; rep from * around—104 (112) sts.

Work 2 rnds even in p1, k7 rib.

NEXT (INC) RND: *P1, M1, k7; rep from * around—117 (126) sts.

Work 2 rnds even in p1, k8 rib.

NEXT (INC) RND: *P1, k8, M1; rep from * around—130 (140) sts.

Continue inc every 6 rnds 5 more times, alternating before knit sts, then after knit sts each time, and knit new sts—195 (210) sts.

Work even in p1, k14 rib until piece measures 12" (30.5 cm).

Work chart rows 1–12 three times, then work rnds 13–16 once.

BO knitwise.

Finishing

Weave in ends. Block to measurements.

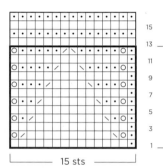

work 3 times

15 sts

	k on RS; p on WS
·	p on RS; k on WS
o	yo
/	k2tog
\	ssk
■	repeat box

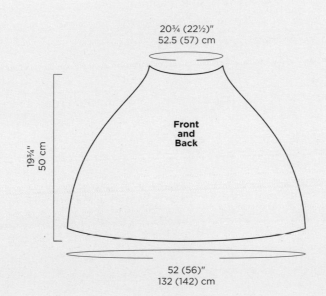

20¾ (22½)"
52.5 (57) cm

Front
and
Back

19¾"
50 cm

52 (56)"
132 (142) cm

Penelope
Moss Stitch Jacket

Although this self-collar jacket features many fine details, it's easy to knit. The front bands and collar are knitted at the same time as the front sections. The sleeves are three-quarter length.

		S	M	L	XL
BUST	in	34½	38	41	44½
	cm	88	96.5	104	113
LENGTH	in	22¼	22¾	23	23½
	cm	56.5	58	58.5	59.5

Yarn Fingering weight (Super fine #1). Shown in: Isager Spinni (100% wool; 667 yd [610 m]/100 g): light brown #7s, 3 (3, 3, 4) skeins. Fingering weight (Superfine #1). Shown in: Isager Alpaca 2 (50% alpaca, 50% merino; 547 yd [500 m]/50 g): light brown #284, 3 (4, 4, 4) skeins.

Needles U.S. size 10 (6 mm): straight needles. Adjust needle size if necessary to obtain the correct gauge.

Notions Stitch markers (m), tapestry needle, five 1¼" (30 mm) buttons.

Gauge 15 sts and 22 rows = 4" (10 cm) in moss st.

Back

CO 65 (71, 77, 83) sts. Work in moss st until piece measures 2¼" (6 cm), ending with a WS row.

NEXT (DEC) ROW: P2tog (or k2tog to maintain patt), work as established to last 2 sts, p2tog (or k2tog)—2 sts dec'd.

Rep dec row every 12 rows twice more—59 (65, 71, 77) sts.

Work even until piece measures 10¼ (10¼, 10¾, 10¾)" (26 [26, 27, 27] cm), ending with a WS row.

NEXT (INC) ROW: Work 1 st, M1, work as established to last st, M1, work 1—2 sts inc'd.

Rep inc row every 8 rows twice more, working new sts into patt—65 (71, 77, 83) sts.

Work even until piece measures 14½" (37 cm), ending with a WS row.

Shape armhole

BO 3 (3, 3, 4) sts at beg of next 2 rows, 2 sts at beg of next 2 rows. Dec 1 st each end every RS row 2 (3, 3, 3) times—51 (55, 61, 65) sts.

Continue even until armhole measures 7 (7½, 7¾, 8¼)" (18 [19, 20, 21] cm).

Shape neck and shoulders

NEXT ROW: Work 14 (16, 18, 20) sts, join a second set of yarns, BO the center 23 (23, 25, 25) sts for neck, work rem 14 (16, 18, 20) sts. Work each side separately.

BO 7 (8, 9, 10) sts at beg of next 4 rows.

Left Front

CO 26 (29, 32, 35) sts. Work in moss st, and *at the same time,* inc 1 st at front edge every other row 9 times and work the new sts into patt. *At the same time,* when piece measures 2¼" (6 cm), end with a WS row.

NEXT (DEC) ROW (RS): Work 1 st, p2tog (or k2tog to maintain patt), work to end—1 st dec'd.

Rep dec row every 12 rows twice more—32 (35, 38, 41) sts.

Work even until piece measures 10¼ (10¼, 10¾, 10¾)" (26 [26, 27, 27] cm), ending with a WS row.

NEXT (INC) ROW: Work 1 st, M1, work as established to end—1 st inc'd.

Rep inc row every 8 rows twice more, working new sts into patt—35 (38, 41, 44) sts.

Work even until piece measures 14½" (37 cm), ending with a WS row.

Shape armhole and front neck

BO 3 (3, 3, 4) sts, work in established patt to last 2 sts, pm, k1, work last st in patt—32 (35, 38, 40) sts.

NEXT ROW: Work 1 st, p1, slm, work in patt to end.

NEXT ROW: BO 2 sts, work in patt to 2 sts before m, k2tog (or p2tog to maintain patt), slm, k1, M1, work rem st—30 (33, 36, 38) sts.

NEXT ROW: Work 2 sts in patt, p1, slm, work in patt to end.

Continue dec 1 st at armhole edge every RS row 2 (3, 3, 3) times and keep st after marker on RS rows (and before marker on WS rows) in St st. *At the same time,* dec 1 st in patt before marker (every 4 rows, then every 2 rows) 6 (6, 7, 7) more times, then every 4 rows 1 (1, 0, 0) more time, and *at the same time,* inc 1 st after St st every RS row 20 (20, 21, 21) more times. *At the same time,* when armhole measures 7 (7½, 7¾, 8¼)" (18 [19, 20, 21] cm), end with a WS row.

Shape shoulder

Continue rem neck and collar shaping, BO 7 (8, 9, 10) sts at beg of next 2 RS rows—21 (21, 22, 22) sts rem.

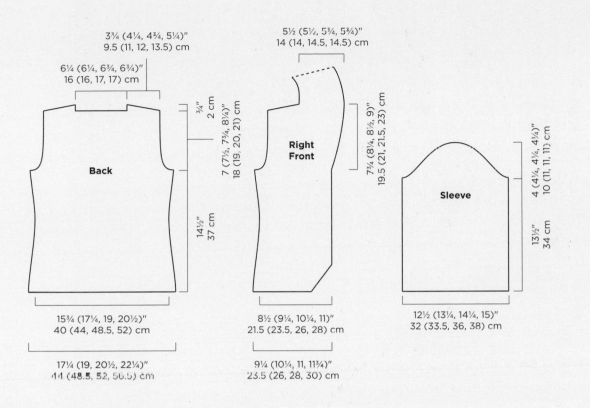

3¾ (4¼, 4¾, 5¼)"
9.5 (11, 12, 13.5) cm

6¼ (6¼, 6¾, 6¾)"
16 (16, 17, 17) cm

¾"
2 cm

Back

7 (7½, 7¾, 8¼)"
18 (19, 20, 21) cm

14½"
37 cm

15¾ (17¼, 19, 20½)"
40 (44, 48.5, 52) cm

17¼ (19, 20½, 22¼)"
44 (48.5, 52, 56.5) cm

5½ (5½, 5¾, 5¾)"
14 (14, 14.5, 14.5) cm

Right Front

7¾ (8¼, 8½, 9)"
19.5 (21, 21.5, 23) cm

8½ (9¼, 10¼, 11)"
21.5 (23.5, 26, 28) cm

9¼ (10¼, 11, 11¾)"
23.5 (26, 28, 30) cm

4 (4¼, 4¼, 4¼)"
10 (11, 11, 11) cm

Sleeve

13½"
34 cm

12½ (13¼, 14¼, 15)"
32 (33.5, 36, 38) cm

Collar

*SHORT-ROW SET (WS): Work 14 (14, 15, 15) sts in moss st, turn, yo, and work back to edge of collar.

Work 2 rows over all sts, working yo together with next st (*Note:* When turning there will be 2 sts next to each other in the same patt st [either knit or purl], the correct pattern will be restored after the next short-row.)

Rep short-row set once more. Work 2 rows over all sts working yo together with next st*.

Rep from * to * until inner (shorter) edge reaches center of back neck. Place collar sts on holder.

Place 5 markers on front edge to mark button placement. Bottom button should be about ½" (1.3 cm) above last inc

shaping front edge and top button about ½" (1.3 cm) below beg of neck/collar shaping, evenly space rem 3 buttons in between.

Right Front

CO 26 (29, 32, 35) sts. Work in moss st, and *at the same time,* inc 1 st at front edge every other row 9 times and work the new sts into patt. *At the same time,* when piece measures 2¼" (6 cm), end with a WS row.

NEXT (DEC) ROW (RS): Work 1 st, p2tog (or k2tog to maintain patt), work to end—1 st dec'd.

Rep dec row every 12 rows twice more—32 (35, 38, 41) sts. *At the same time,* when piece measures about ½" (1.3 cm) above last inc, end with a WS row

NEXT (BUTTONHOLE) ROW (RS): Work 2 sts, BO 2 for buttonhole, work in established patt to end.

NEXT ROW: CO 2 sts over buttonhole gap.

Work rem buttonholes as marked, then work even until piece measures 10¼ (10¼, 10¾, 10¾)" (26 [26, 27, 27] cm), ending with a WS row.

NEXT (INC) ROW: Work as established to last st, M1, work 1—1 st inc'd.

Rep inc row every 8 rows twice more, working new sts into patt—35 (38, 41, 44) sts.

Work even until piece measures 14½" (37 cm), ending with a RS row.

Shape armhole and front neck

BO 3 (3, 3, 4) sts, work in established patt to last 2 sts, pm, p1, work last st in patt—32 (35, 38, 40) sts.

NEXT ROW: Work 1 st, M1, k1, slm, work in patt to end—1 st inc'd.

NEXT ROW: BO 2 sts, work in patt to 2 sts before m, k2tog (or p2tog to maintain patt), slm, p1, work rem 2 sts—30 (33, 36, 38) sts.

NEXT ROW: Work 2 sts in patt, M1, k1, slm, work in patt to end—1 st inc'd.

Continue dec 1 st at armhole edge every WS row 2 (3, 3, 3) times and keep st before marker on RS rows (and after marker on WS rows) in St st. *At the same time,* dec 1 st in patt after markers (every 4 rows, then every 2 rows) 6 (6, 7, 7) more times, then every 4 rows 1 (1, 0, 0) more time, and *at the same time,* inc 1 st before St st every RS row 19 (19, 20, 20) more times. *At the same time,* when armhole measures 7 (7½, 7¾, 8¼)" (18 [19, 20, 21] cm), end with a RS row.

Shape shoulder

Continue rem neck and collar shaping, BO 7 (8, 9, 10) sts at beg of next 2 WS rows—21 (21, 22, 22) sts rem.

Collar

*SHORT-ROW SET (RS): Work 14 (14, 15, 15) sts in moss st, turn, yo, and work back to edge of collar.

Work 2 rows over all sts, working yo together with next st.

Rep short-row set once more. Work 2 rows over all sts working yo together with next st*.

Rep from * to * until inner (shorter) edge reaches center of back neck. Place collar sts on holder.

After completing right front, place sts from the two halves of the collar with RS facing RS and join the sets of sts with three-needle bind-off

Sleeves

CO 47 (50, 53, 56) sts. Work in moss st until piece measures 13½" (34 cm), ending with a WS row.

Shape cap

BO 3 (3, 3, 4) sts at beg of next 2 rows, 2 sts at beg of next 2 (2, 4, 4) rows. Dec 1 st each end every RS row 5 (6, 5, 5) times. BO 2 sts at beg of next 4 rows, 3 sts at beg of next 4 (4, 4, 2) rows, then 4 sts at beg of next 0 (0, 0, 2) rows—7 (8, 9, 8) sts. BO rem sts.

Finishing

Weave in ends. Block pieces to finished measurements.

Sew shoulder seams. Seam collar to back neck. Sew sleeve and side seams. Sew in sleeves. Sew buttons to left front opposite buttonholes.

Cable
Patterns

By crossing stitches in front of or behind each other, you can create the most fantastic three-dimensional patterns. Cable patterns are typically used for the classic chunky Aran sweaters, but they also look great worked in elegant fine yarns.

Viola
Top with Cap Sleeves

This ultrafeminine vest is knit with the lightest wool yarn. The little cap sleeves are made with cables that become wider and wider toward the top. The increases are hidden in the cable twists and are made on the same row as the cable crossings.

		S	M	L	XL
BUST	in	34¾	37¾	41	43½
	cm	88	96	106	112
LENGTH	in	24	24½	25¼	25½
	cm	61	62	64	65

notes:

The top is knit with a special, very lofty yarn. The wool fiber is contained within a tulle fabric net. If you want to knit with a different (more generally available) yarn at the same gauge, you will need almost twice the number of balls of yarn.

Yarn Chunky weight (Bulky #5). Shown in: Gepard Puno (68% alpaca, 22% mixed synthetic fiber, 10% merino wool; 120 yd [110 m]/50 g): beige #1315, 3 (4, 4, 5) balls.

Needles U.S. size 11 (8 mm): straight and 16" (40 cm) circular (cir). Adjust needle size if necessary to obtain the correct gauge.

Notions Stitch markers (m), cable needle (cn), stitch holders, tapestry needle.

Gauge 12 sts and 18 rows = 4" (10 cm) in St st.

Left Cable

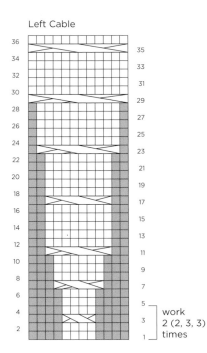

Right Cable

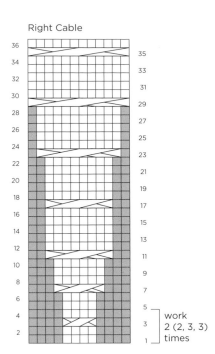

work
2 (2, 3, 3)
times

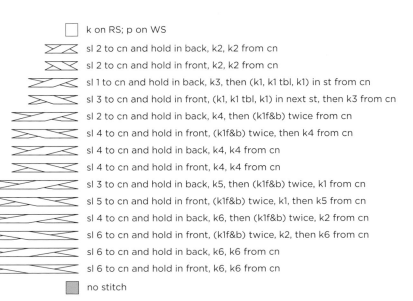

	k on RS; p on WS
	sl 2 to cn and hold in back, k2, k2 from cn
	sl 2 to cn and hold in front, k2, k2 from cn
	sl 1 to cn and hold in back, k3, then (k1, k1 tbl, k1) in st from cn
	sl 3 to cn and hold in front, (k1, k1 tbl, k1) in next st, then k3 from cn
	sl 2 to cn and hold in back, k4, then (k1f&b) twice from cn
	sl 4 to cn and hold in front, (k1f&b) twice, then k4 from cn
	sl 4 to cn and hold in back, k4, k4 from cn
	sl 4 to cn and hold in front, k4, k4 from cn
	sl 3 to cn and hold in back, k5, then (k1f&b) twice, k1 from cn
	sl 5 to cn and hold in front, (k1f&b) twice, k1, then k5 from cn
	sl 4 to cn and hold in back, k6, then (k1f&b) twice, k2 from cn
	sl 6 to cn and hold in front, (k1f&b) twice, k2, then k6 from cn
	sl 6 to cn and hold in back, k6, k6 from cn
	sl 6 to cn and hold in front, k6, k6 from cn
	no stitch

Back

CO 57 (63, 67, 71) sts. Work 5 rows in k1, p1 rib, ending with a WS row.

Continue in St st until piece measures 5½" (14 cm), ending with a WS row.

NEXT (DEC) ROW (RS): K2, k2tog, knit to last 4 sts, ssk, k2—2 sts dec'd.

Rep dec row every 8 (8, 10, 10) rows twice more—51 (57, 61, 65) sts.

Work even until piece measures 11¾ (12¼, 12¼, 12½)" (30 [31, 31, 32.5] cm), ending with a WS row.

NEXT (INC) ROW (RS): K1, M1, knit to last st, M1, K1—2 sts inc'd.

Rep inc row every 4 rows twice more—57 (63, 67, 71) sts.

Work even until piece measures 15 (15½, 15½, 15¾)" (38 [39, 39, 40] cm), ending with a WS row.

Shape armhole

NEXT ROW (RS): BO 3 (4, 3, 4) sts (1 st rem on right needle), k4, p1, knit to last 9 (10, 9, 10) sts, p1, k8 (9, 8, 9)—54 (59, 64, 67) sts.

NEXT ROW: BO 3 (4, 3, 4) sts (1 st rem on right needle), p4, k1, purl to last 6 sts, k1, p4, k1—51 (55, 61, 63) sts.

NEXT ROW: K1 (edge st), work Row 1 of Right Cable chart over next 4 sts, p1, place marker (pm), k2tog, knit to last 8 sts, pm, ssk, p1, work Row 1 of Left Cable chart over next 4 sts, k1 (edge st)—2 sts dec'd.

ROW AND ALL FOLL WS ROWS: K1 (edge st), purl to 1 st before m, k1, slm, purl to m, slm, k1, purl to last st, k1 (edge st).

NEXT ROW (RS): K1 (edge st), work Row 3 over next 4 sts, p1, slm, k2tog; knit to last 8 sts, ssk, slm, p1, work

Row 3 over next 4 sts, k1 (edge st)—2 sts dec'd.

Keeping edge sts in garter st, continue cable charts and dec between markers every RS row 2 (2, 4, 4) more times—43 (47, 49, 51) sts; 31 (35, 37, 39) sts rem between m, and 4 sts in each cable.

Working even over sts between m, continue cable charts through Row 31—59 (63, 65, 67) sts; 31 (35, 37, 39) sts between m, and 12 sts in each cable.

Shape neck and shoulders

NEXT ROW (WS): Work 20 (22, 22, 23) sts, turn, place rem 39 (41, 43, 44) sts on holder.

Continue Left Cable chart and work 4 more rows. Place left shoulder sts on holder.

Return first 20 (22, 22, 23) sts to needle for right shoulder, leaving center 19 (19, 21, 21) sts on holder for back neck. Join yarn to beg with a WS row. Work rem 5 rows of Right Cable chart. Place right shoulder sts on holder.

Front

Work as for back through Row 11 of cable charts.

Shape neck

NEXT ROW (WS): Work 21 (21, 23, 24) sts, place center 9 (9, 11, 11) sts on holder for front neck, join a second ball of yarn and work to end. Work each side separately and continue cable charts.

NEXT (DEC) ROW (RS): Work to 3 sts before neck, ssk, k1; k1, k2tog, work to end—1 st dec'd each shoulder.

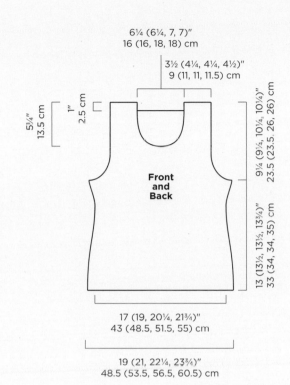

6¼ (6¼, 7, 7)"
16 (16, 18, 18) cm

3½ (4¼, 4¼, 4½)"
9 (11, 11, 11.5) cm

5¼" 13.5 cm

1" 2.5 cm

9¼ (9¼, 10¼, 10¼)"
23.5 (23.5, 26, 26) cm

Front and Back

13 (13½, 13½, 13¾)"
33 (34, 34, 35) cm

17 (19, 20¼, 21¾)"
43 (48.5, 51.5, 55) cm

19 (21, 22¼, 23¾)"
48.5 (53.5, 56.5, 60.5) cm

Rep dec row every RS row 4 times more—16 (18, 18, 19) sts each shoulder.

Continue through Row 36 of cable charts—20 (22, 22, 23) sts each shoulder.

Join shoulders using three-needle bind-off.

Finishing

Weave in ends. Block pieces to finished measurements.

Sew side seams.

Neckband

With cir needle and RS facing, beg at left shoulder seam, pick up and k12 sts along left front neck, k9 (9, 11, 11) sts from front holder, 17 sts along right neck, k19 (19, 21, 21) sts from back holder, 5 sts along left back neck—62 (62, 66, 66) sts along neck. Join to work in the rnd. Pm for beg of rnd. Work 4 rnds in k1, p1 rib. BO in ribbing.

Lea & Lola
One Sweater, Two Lengths

Two-in-one: The short bolero and the long sweater are exactly the same except for their lengths. Both are pleated to gather in the fabric at the back—a delightful detail. The garments are knit with an ultrafine and light yarn so even the long sweater weighs little more than 10.5 ounces (300 g).

		S	M	L	XL
BUST	in	33	36¼	39¼	42½
	cm	84	92	100	108
TOTAL LENGTH					
Bolero	in	16	16¾	17½	17¾
	cm	40.5	42.5	44.5	45
Duster	in	27¼	28	28¾	29
	cm	69	71	73	73.5

note:

Many other yarns are available that will work equally well at this gauge, for example, Mini Alpaca and Mini Duett from Sandnes Garn and Semilla Fino and Silkbloom Fino from BC Garn. If the substitute you choose has fewer yards (meters) than the recommended yarn, don't forget to buy extra.

Yarn Fingering weight (Superfine #1). Shown in: Isager Alpaca 2 (50% alpaca, 50% merino wool; 547 yd [500 m]/100 g): #015 peach, 2 (2, 2, 2) skeins for bolero, and #012 gray-green, 3 (3, 3, 4) skeins for duster.

Needles U.S. size 2.5 (3 mm): straight. U.S. size 4 (3.5 mm): straight and 32" (80 cm) circular (cir). Adjust needle sizes if necessary to obtain the correct gauge.

Notions 2 cable needles (cn) or double-pointed needles (dpn), stitch holders, 4 locking markers (m), seven ⅝–¾" (16–19 mm) buttons.

Gauge 27 sts and 36 rows = 4" (10 cm) in St st on larger needles.

STITCH GUIDE

3/3 LC *(3 over 3 left cross cable)*
Sl 3 sts onto cn and hold in front, k3, k3 from cn.

3/3 RC *(3 over 3 right cross cable)*
Sl 3 sts onto cn and hold in back, k3, k3 from cn.

LEFT PLEAT
(pleat folding to the left)
Worked over 18 sts: Place the next 6 sts on first cn and hold in front, place the next 6 sts on a second cn and hold in front. Arrange the two cable needles in front of the left-hand needle with the left-hand needle in back, the first cn in front and the second cn between (the needles form a zigzag). *Knit the first st of each cn/needle together (k3tog); repeat from * 5 more times—12 sts decreased.

RIGHT PLEAT
(pleat folding to the right)
Worked over 18 sts: Place the next 6 sts on first cn and hold in back, place the next 6 sts on a second cn and hold in back. Arrange the two cable needles in back of the left-hand needle with the left-hand needle in front, the second cn behind the left-hand needle and the first cn behind the second cn (the needles form a zigzag). *Knit the first st of each cn/needle together (k3tog); rep from * 5 more times—12 sts decreased.

note:

Instructions for both the bolero and duster are included in the pattern and are separated by a slash (/): numbers before the slash pertain to the bolero, and numbers after the slash refer to the duster.

Depending on the size of button used, buttonholes may need to be either 2 or 3 stitches. Work a sample band along the side of your gauge swatch to test the size of the buttonholes.

Back Cables

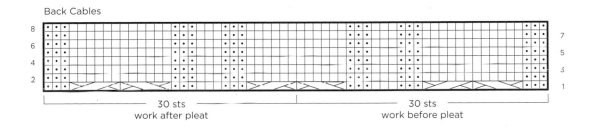

8
6
4
2

7
5
3
1

|———— 30 sts ————|
work after pleat

|———— 30 sts ————|
work before pleat

Double Cable

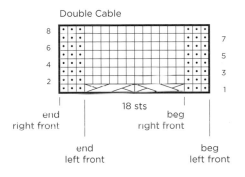

8
6
4
2

7
5
3
1

| 18 sts |

end
right front

beg
right front

end
left front

beg
left front

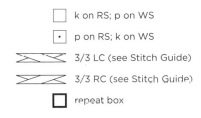

☐   k on RS; p on WS

⊡   p on RS; k on WS

⧖   3/3 LC (see Stitch Guide)

⧗   3/3 RC (see Stitch Guide)

▢   repeat box

Back

With larger needles, CO 161 (171, 183, 193) sts.

ROW 1 (WS): K1 (edge st), p1, (k1, p1) to last st, k1 (edge st).

ROW 2: K1 (edge st), (k1, p1) to last 2 sts, k1, k1 (edge st).

Work 5 more rows in rib as established, ending with a WS row.

NEXT (SET-UP) ROW (RS): K1 (edge st), knit next 36 (41, 47, 52) sts and dec 4 sts evenly spaced across these sts, work right half of Row 1 of Back Cables chart over next 30 sts, purl next 27 sts and dec 3 sts evenly spaced across these sts, work left half of Row 1 of Back Cables chart over next 30 sts, knit next 36 (41, 47, 52) sts and dec 4 sts evenly spaced across these sts, k1 (edge st)—150 (160, 172, 182) sts.

NEXT ROW: K1 (edge st), p32 (37, 43, 48), work first half of Row 2 of Back Cables chart over next 30 sts, k24, work second half of Row 2 of Back Cables chart over next 30 sts, purl to last st, k1 (edge st).

Continue patt as established, keeping the edge sts in garter st until piece measures 7 / 18¼" (18 / 46.5 cm), ending with a WS row.

BO 10 (11, 13, 14) sts at the beg of next 2 rows—130 (138, 146, 154) sts. Place rem sts on holder.

Left Front

With larger needles, CO 66 (70, 76, 82) sts.

ROW 1 (WS): K1 (edge st), p1, (k1, p1) to last 2 sts, k1, k1 (edge st).

Rep last row 6 more times, ending with a WS row.

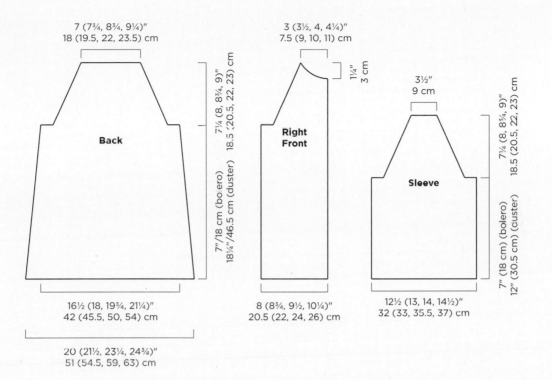

Back

7 (7¾, 8¾, 9¼)"
18 (19.5, 22, 23.5) cm

7¼ (8, 8¾, 9)"
18.5 (20.5, 22, 23) cm

7"/18 cm (bolero)
18¼"/46.5 cm (duster)

16½ (18, 19¾, 21¼)"
42 (45.5, 50, 54) cm

20 (21½, 23¼, 24¾)"
51 (54.5, 59, 63) cm

Right Front

3 (3½, 4, 4¼)"
7.5 (9, 10, 11) cm

1¼"
3 cm

8 (8¾, 9½, 10¼)"
20.5 (22, 24, 26) cm

Sleeve

3½"
9 cm

7¼ (8, 8¾, 9)"
18.5 (20.5, 22, 23) cm

7" (18 cm) (bolero)
12" (30.5 cm) (duster)

12½ (13, 14, 14½)"
32 (33, 35.5, 37) cm

Next (set-up) Row: (RS) K1 (edge st), k49 (53, 59, 65) sts and dec 6 (5, 5, 6) sts evenly spaced across these sts, work Row 1 of Double Cable chart over next 15 sts, k1 (edge st)—60 (65, 71, 76) sts.

NEXT ROW: K1 (edge st), work Row 2 of Double Cable chart over next 15 sts, purl to last st, k1 (edge st).

Continue in patt as established, keeping the edge sts in garter st until piece measures 7 / 18¼" (18 / 46.5 cm), ending with same WS row as back before armhole BO.

BO 10 (11, 13, 14) sts at beg of next row—50 (54, 58, 62) sts.

Work 1 row even. Place rem sts on a holder.

Right Front

With larger needles, CO 66 (70, 76, 82) sts.

ROW 1 (WS): K1 (edge st), (k1, p1) to last st, k1 (edge st).

ROW 2: K1 (edge st), (k1, p1) to last st, k1 (edge st).

Work 5 more rows in rib as established, ending with a WS row.

Next (set-up) Row (RS): K1 (edge st), work Double Cable chart over next 15 sts, k49 (53, 59, 65) sts and dec 6 (5, 5, 6) sts evenly spaced across these sts, k1 (edge st)—60 (65, 71, 76) sts.

NEXT ROW: K1 (edge st), p43 (48, 54, 59), work Row 2 of Double Cable chart over next 15 sts, k1 (edge st).

Continue in patt as established, keeping the edge sts in garter st until piece measures 7 / 18¼" (18 / 46.5 cm), ending with same RS row of chart that sts were bound-off for left front.

BO 10 (11, 13, 14) sts at beg of next row—50 (54, 58, 62) sts. Place rem sts on a holder.

Sleeves

With larger needles, CO 102 (106, 112, 116) sts.

ROW 1 (WS): K1 (edge st), p1, (k1, p1) to last 2 sts, k1, k1 (edge st).

Rep last row 6 more times, ending with a WS row.

NEXT (SET-UP) ROW (RS): K1 (edge st), k41 (43, 46, 48) and dec 5 sts evenly spaced across these st, work Row 1 of Double Cable chart over next 18 sts, k41 (43, 46, 48) and dec 5 sts evenly spaced across these sts, k1 (edge st)—92 (96, 102, 106) sts.

NEXT ROW: K1 (edge st), p36 (38, 41, 43), work Row 2 of Double Cable chart over next 18 sts, purl to last st, k1 (edge st).

Continue in patt as established until piece measures about 7 / 12" (18 / 30.5 cm), ending with same WS row as back before armhole BO.

BO 10 (11, 13, 14) sts at beg of next 2 rows—72 (74, 76, 78) sts. Place rem sts on a holder.

Yoke

With RS facing, place sts on cir needle as foll: 50 (54, 58, 62) left front sts, 72 (74, 76, 78) sleeve sts, 130 (138, 146, 154) back sts, 72 (74, 76, 78) sleeve sts, then 50 (54, 58, 62) right front sts—374 (394, 414, 434) sts.

NEXT (SET-UP) ROW (RS): *Work as established to 1 st before armhole, k2tog; rep from * 3 more times, work to end—370 (390, 410, 430) sts. Place locking markers (pm) on the 4 dec sts, and move them up as work progresses.

Work 1 row even, keeping marked sts in St st.

NEXT (RAGLAN DEC) ROW (RS): *Work to 2 sts before marked st, k2tog, k1, ssk; rep from * 3 more times, then work to end of row—8 sts dec'd.

Rep raglan dec row (every 2 rows, every 4 rows) 8 (9, 10, 10) times, then every other row 1 (0, 0, 1) more time. *At the same time,* when armhole measures about ¾" (2 cm), form pleats on a RS row as foll: work to 6 sts before reverse St st at center of back, make Left Pleat (see Stitch Guide), make Right Pleat (see Stitch Guide), work to end—24 sts dec. *Note:* Pleats should not be worked on a cable crossing row; adjust placement of pleats if necessary by working more or fewer rows before forming pleats. When raglan dec are complete, 202 (214, 218, 230) sts rem.

Without working, sl first 2 sts to right needle, pass edge st over 2nd st and off needle; rep at opposite end of needle—200 (212, 216, 228) sts. End with a WS row.

Shape neck

Continue raglan dec as established.

NEXT ROW (RS): Work first 7 (8, 9, 10) sts and place on holder, work to last 7 (8, 9, 10) sts, place last 7 (8, 9, 10) sts on holder.

BO 3 sts at beg of every row and continue raglan dec as established until 4 more raglan dec have been worked. *Note:* Work last raglan dec on sleeves and back only. Place rem 128 (138, 140, 150) sts on holder.

Finishing

Weave in ends. Block pieces to finished measurements.

Sew sleeve and side seams. Seam underarm seams.

Buttonband

With smaller needles and RS facing, beg at neck edge and, pick up and knit sts 3 sts for every 4 rows along left front edge to bottom edge.

Work in k1, p1 rib for 7 rows. BO in ribbing.

Buttonhole band

With smaller needles and RS facing, beg a bottom edge and pick up and knit 3 sts for every 4 rows along right front edge to neck.

Work in k1, p1 rib for 2 rows.

Pm for 6 buttons along band, center bottom marker along bottom rib, then evenly space rem markers along edge (last buttonhole will be worked in center of neckband).

NEXT (BUTTONHOLE) ROW (WS): *Work to 1 st before m, BO 2 or 3 sts for buttonhole: rep from * 5 more times, then work to end.

NEXT ROW: CO 2 or 3 sts over gap left by buttonholes.

Work 3 rows even. BO in ribbing.

Neckband

With smaller needles and RS facing, pick up and k5 sts along edge of front band, knit sts from front holder and dec 2 (3, 3, 4) sts over these sts, pick up and k13 (13, 14, 12) sts along right neck edge, knit sts from neck holder and dec 4 sts over each double cable, pick up and k12 (12, 13, 11) sts along left neck to holder, knit sts from rem front holder and dec 2 (3, 3, 4) sts over these sts, pick up and k5 sts along edge of front band—153 (163, 169, 175) sts.

ROW 1 (WS): P1, *k1, p1; rep from * to end.

ROW 2: *K1, p1; rep from * to last st, k1.

ROW 3 (BUTTONHOLE): P1, k1, BO 2 or 3 for buttonhole, work to end.

ROW 4: CO 2 or 3 sts over gap left by buttonhole.

Work 3 more rows even. BO in ribbing.

Sew buttons to left front opposite buttonholes.

Petra
Seed Stitch Wrist Warmers

When it isn't too cold outside, wrist warmers are all you need to keep your wrists and hands warm. These are knit with the finest wool and silk yarn that really makes the seed stitch look like little pearls.

		one size
HAND CIRCUMFERENCE	in	6¼
	cm	16
LENGTH	in	9½
	cm	24

Yarn Sportweight (Fine #2). Shown in: BC Garn Silkbloom Fino (55% merino wool, 45% silk; 219 yd [200 m]/50 g): mustard yellow #ix21, 1 ball.

Needles U.S. size 2.5 (3 mm): set of 5 double-pointed needles (dpn). Adjust needle size if necessary to obtain the correct gauge.

Notions Stitch marker, stitch holder, cable needle (cn), tapestry needle.

Gauge 27 sts and 50 rows = 4″ (10 cm) in seed st.

Stitch Guide

2/1 LC *(2 over 1 left cross)*
Sl 2 sts to cn and hold in front, k1, k2 from cn.

2/1 LPC *(2 over 1 left purl cross)*
Sl 2 sts to cn and hold in front, p1, k2 from cn.

2/1 RC *(2 over 1 right cross)*
Sl 1 st to cn and hold in back, k2, k1 from cn.

2/1 RPC *(2 over 1 right purl cross)*
Sl 1 st to cn and hold in back, k2, p1 from cn.

2/2 LC *(2 over 2 left cross)*
Sl 2 sts to cn and hold in front, k2, k2 from cn.

2/2 RC *(2 over 2 right cross)*
Sl 2 sts to cn and hold in back, k2, k2 from cn.

SEED STITCH
(multiple of 2 sts)

RND 1: *K1, p1; rep from * around.

RND 2: *P1, k1; rep from * around.

Rep Rnds 1 and 2 for patt.

Right Wrist Warmer

CO 50 sts. Divide sts over 4 dpn with 12 sts on 2 of the needles and 13 sts on 2 needles. Join, being careful not to twist sts. Place marker (pm) for beg of rnd.

Work k1, p1 rib for 2¾" (7 cm).

NEXT (SET-UP) RND: Work Row 1 of Cable chart over first 22 sts, work seed st over rem 28 sts and adjust sts on needles so center 12 sts of Cable chart are on one needle.

Work even until piece measures 7" (18 cm).

NEXT RND: Work 38 sts as established, place next 9 sts on holder for thumb, work rem 3 sts.

NEXT RND: CO 9 new sts over thumb gap.

Continue even in pattern until chart has been worked twice (piece measures about 9½" (24 cm). BO in patt.

Thumb

Place thumb sts on dpn, pick up and knit 1 st at side of opening, 11 sts along CO edge above thumbhole, and pick up and knit 1 st at side of opening—22 sts.

Join and pm for beg of rnd.

NEXT (DEC) RND: K11, k2tog, k5, k2tog, k2—20 sts.

Knit 3 rnds even.

NEXT (DEC) RND: K13, k2tog, knit to end—1 st dec.

Rep last 4 rnds once more—18 sts.

Work even until thumb measures 1¾–2" (4–5 cm). BO all sts.

Left Wrist Warmer

Work same as for right wrist warmer until piece measures 7" (18 cm).

Next rnd: Work 28 sts as established, place next 9 sts on holder for thumb, work rem 13 sts.

Next rnd: CO 9 new sts over thumb gap.

Complete left same as right wrist warmer.

Weave in ends.

Cable

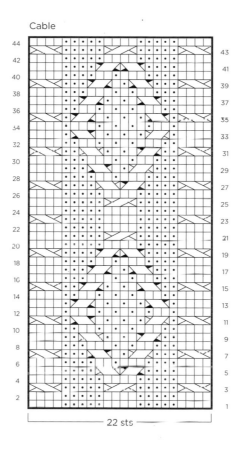

44
42
40
38
36
34
32
30
28
26
24
22
20
18
16
14
12
10
8
6
4
2

43
41
39
37
35
33
31
29
27
25
23
21
19
17
15
13
11
9
7
5
3
1

|—— 22 sts ——|

☐ k on RS; p on WS

⊡ p on RS; k on WS

2/1 LC (see Stitch Guide)

2/1 RC (see Stitch Guide)

2/1 LPC (see Stitch Guide)

2/1 RPC (see Stitch Guide)

2/2 LC (see Stitch Guide)

2/2 RC (see Stitch Guide)

▢ repeat box

Wilma
Little Cabled Vest

This smart and close-fitting little vest sports classic cable and twist patterns. All the stitches are shown on the chart so this vest is a good project for anyone ready to throw themselves into cables. Wear the vest over a flowing dress or skirt.

		S / M	L / XL
BACK	in	17	19¼
	cm	43	49
LENGTH	in	13½	15
	cm	34	38

Yarn Worsted weight (Medium #4) for size S/M. Shown in: Wilfert's Tweed (80% new wool, 20% polymaid; 115 yd [105 m]/50 g): brown #62, 3 balls. Aran weight (Medium #4) for size L/XL. Shown in: Rowan Felted Tweed Aran (50% merino wool, 25% alpaca, 25% viscose; 95 yd [87 m]/50 g); cork #721, 4 balls.

Needles Size S/M: U.S. size 7 (4.5 mm): straight, 16" (40 cm) and 32" (80 cm) long circular (cir); U.S. size 9 (5.5 mm): straight. Adjust needle sizes if necessary to obtain the correct gauge. Size L/XL: U.S. size 8 (5 mm): straight, 16" (40 cm) and 32" (80 cm) long circular; U.S. size 10 (6 mm): straight. Adjust needle sizes if necessary to obtain the correct gauge.

Notions Cable needle (cn), stitch holders, tapestry needle.

Gauge 17 sts and 24 rows = 4" (10 cm) in St st using larger needles and Wilfert's Tweed for size S/M; 15 sts and 21½ rows = 4" (10 cm) in St st using larger needles and Rowan Felted Tweed Aran for size L/XL.

> **note:**
>
> The finished measurements will vary depending on the thickness or fineness of the yarn and needles used. The vest is worked following the chart, with the same stitch count for both sizes. If you want a larger vest, you can choose heavier yarn, and, vice versa, if you want a smaller, child's size vest, use finer yarn.
>
> When picking up stitches along the lower edges of the front, make sure to pick up stitches close together along curved edges so edging won't curl.

STICH GUIDE

2/1 LPC *(2 over 1 left purl cross)*
Sl 2 sts to cn and hold in front, p1, k2 from cn.

2/1 RPC *(2 over 1 right purl cross)*
Sl 1 st to cn and hold in back, k2, p1 from cn.

2/2 LC *(2 over 2 left cross)*
Sl 2 sts to cn and hold in front, k2, k2 from cn.

Back

With smaller needles for your size, CO 78 sts. Knit 4 rows.

Change to larger needles for your size. Continue in Back Chart through Row 34.

Shape armholes

BO 4 sts at beg of next 2 rows, 2 sts at beg of next 6 rows, then 1 st at beg of next 2 rows—56 sts rem. Work even through Row 75; armhole should measure about 6¼ (7¾)" (16 [20] cm).

Shape neck

NEXT ROW: Work 16 sts as established, place next 24 sts on marker for neck, join a second ball of yarn and work rem 16 sts. Work each side separately.

Work 2 rows even. Place rem shoulder sts on holders.

Left Front

With larger needles for your size, CO 23 sts.

SET-UP ROW (WS): K2, p4, k5, p2, k3, p4, k3.

Continue in Left Front chart and CO at end of every RS row 2 sts once, 3 sts once, 1 st 4 times, then 1 st every 6 rows 2 times—34 sts. Work even through Row 34.

Shape armhole

BO at beg of RS rows 4 sts once, then 2 sts 3 times—24 sts.

Work 1 row even.

Shape neck

DEC ROW 1 (RS): BO 1 st, work to last 2 sts, ssk—22 sts.

Work 3 rows even.

DEC ROW 2: Work to last 2 sts, ssk—1 st dec'd.

Rep dec row 2 (every 6 rows, then every 4 rows) twice more, then every 6 rows once more, working dec as ssk or ssp to maintain patt—16 sts.

Continue through end of chart. Place rem sts on holder.

Right Front

With larger needles for your size, CO 23 sts.

SET-UP ROW (WS): K3, p4, k3, p2, k5, p4, k2.

Continue in Right Front chart and CO at beg of every RS row 2 sts once, 3 sts once, 1 st 4 times, then 1 st every 6 rows 2 times—34 sts. Work even through Row 35.

Shape armhole

BO at beg of WS rows 4 sts once, then 2 sts 3 times—24 sts.

Shape neck

NEXT (DEC) ROW (RS): K2tog, work in established patt to end—1 st dec'd.

NEXT ROW: BO 1 st, then work to end—22 sts.

Work 2 rows even.

Rep dec row next row, (every 6 rows, then every 4 rows) twice more, then every 6 rows once more, working dec as k2tog or p2tog to maintain patt—16 sts.

Continue through end of chart. Place rem sts on holder.

Finishing

Weave in ends. Join shoulders using three-needle bind-off.

Armhole edging

With smaller needles for your size and RS facing, pick up and knit 74 sts along armhole.

Knit 3 rows. BO all sts knitwise.

Front and neck edging

With cir needle and RS facing, beg at bottom of right front, pick up and k20 sts along lower edge of right front, 38 sts to beg of neck shaping, 28 sts along right neck to shoulder, knit sts from holder at back neck and k2tog at center of each cable, 28 sts along left neck to bottom of neck opening, 38 sts to bottom edge, then 20 sts along lower edge of left front to side edge—192 sts.

Knit 3 rows. BO all sts knitwise.

Sew side seams.

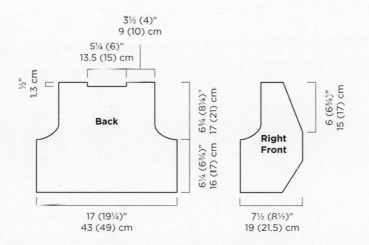

Back chart

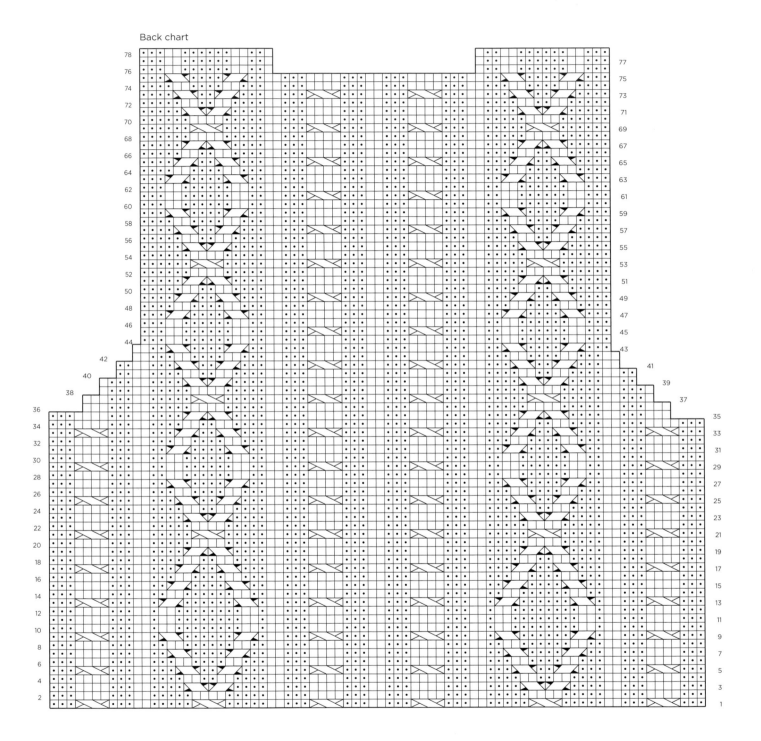

Right Front chart

Left Front chart

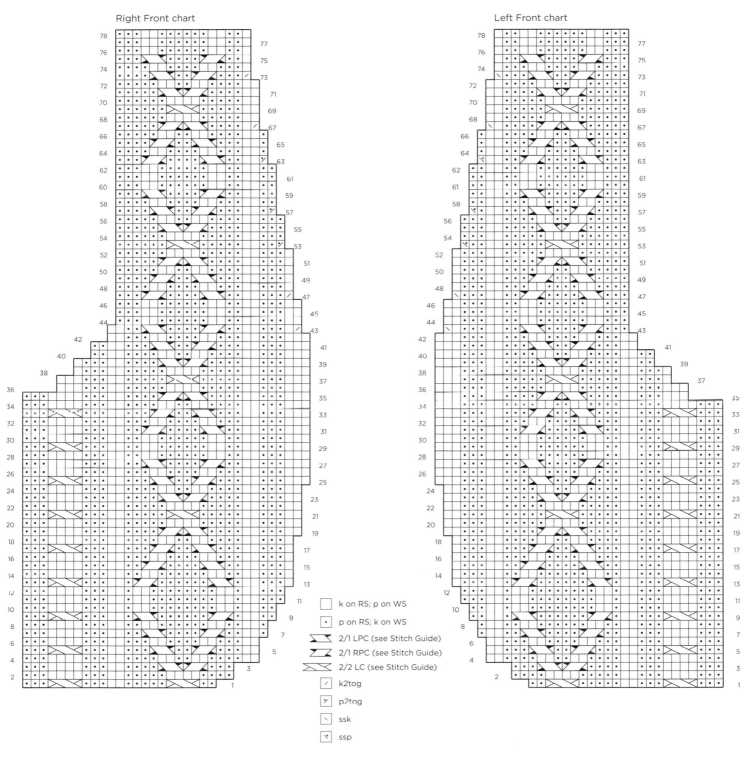

k on RS; p on WS

• p on RS; k on WS

2/1 LPC (see Stitch Guide)

2/1 RPC (see Stitch Guide)

2/2 LC (see Stitch Guide)

k2tog

p2tog

ssk

ssp

Amanda
Classic Cable Sweater

This short, classic raglan sweater has fine cable patterns in the Aran style. It's knit with a light wool tweed yarn so the sweater won't be thick and heavy even with the dense patterning.

		S	M	L	XL
BUST	in	33	35	38	40
	cm	84	89	96.5	101.5
LENGTH	in	21¾	22	22	22½
	cm	55	56	56	57

note:
If you don't want a tweed yarn for your sweater, Madonna from Permin is a good substitute.

Yarn Worsted weight (Medium #4). Shown in: Grignasco Loden (50% wool, 25% viscose, 25% alpaca; 120 yd [110 m]/50 g): light gray #591, 9 (10, 11, 12) balls.

Needles U.S. size 7 (4.5 mm): straight. U.S. size 8 (5 mm): straight and 32" (80 cm) circular (cir). Adjust needle sizes if necessary to obtain the correct gauge.

Notions 2 cable needles (cn), stitch holders, 4 removable markers or safety pins, six ¾" (20 mm) buttons.

Gauge 27½ sts and 28 rows = 4" (10 cm) in Honeycomb patt on larger needles; 13 sts of Diamond Cable = 2½" (6.5 cm) wide.

¾" (2 cm), make buttonhole over next RS row as foll: work 4 sts, BO 2 sts for buttonhole, work to end. On next row CO 2 sts over buttonhole gap.

NEXT ROW: Work 10 (12, 10, 12) sts, *M1, work 10 (10, 12, 12) sts; rep from * twice more, M1, work 4 (6, 6, 8) sts, CO 1 st, place rem 9 sts on holder for buttonhole band—49 (53, 57, 61) sts.

Change to larger needles.

ROW 1 (RS): K1 (edge st), beg chart as shown and work Row 1 of Body chart over next 47 (51, 55, 59) sts, k1 (edge st).

ROW 2: K1 (edge st), beg as shown for your size and work Row 2 of Cable chart over next 47 (51, 55, 59) sts, k1 (edge st).

Keeping edge sts in garter st, continue chart until piece measures 14¼" (36 cm), ending with same RS row as first armhole BO on back.

BO 10 (10, 14, 14) sts at beg of next row—39 (43, 43, 47) sts. Place rem sts on a holder.

Sleeves

With smaller needles, CO 50 (50, 58, 58) sts.

ROW 1 (WS): K1 (edge st), p1, *k1, p1; rep from * to last st, k1 (edge st).

ROW 2: K1 (edge st), *k1, p1; rep from * to last 2 sts, k1, k1 (edge st).

Rep Rows 1 and 2 until rib measures about 2¾" (7 cm), ending with a RS row.

NEXT (INC) ROW (WS): Work 7 (7, 8, 8) sts, *M1, work 6 (6, 7, 7) sts; rep from * 5 more times, M1, work to end—57 (57, 65, 65) sts.

Change to larger needles.

NEXT (SET-UP) ROW (RS): K1 (edge st), beg as shown for your size and work Row 1 of Sleeve chart to last st, k1 (edge st).

Keeping edge sts in garter st, work in established patt until piece measures 3½" (9cm), ending with a WS row.

NEXT (INC) ROW (RS): K1 (edge st), M1, work to last st, M1, k1 (edge st)—2 sts inc'd.

Rep inc row every 8 rows 11 more times, working new sts in honeycomb patt as number of sts permit—81 (81, 89, 89) sts. Work even until piece measures about 17¼" (44 cm), ending with same WS chart row as back before armhole.

BO 10 (10, 14, 14) sts at at beg of next 2 rows—61 sts rem for all sizes. Place rem sts on a holder.

Yoke

With RS facing, place sts for all pieces on cir needle as foll: Right front, sleeve, back, sleeve, left front—282 (298, 298, 314) sts.

NEXT (SET-UP) ROW (RS): Work as established to last st of right front, k2tog, work to last st of sleeve, k2tog, work to last st of back, k2tog, work to last st of sleeve, k2tog, work to end—278 (294, 294, 310) sts. Place marker (pm) on dec sts.

NEXT ROW: *Work to marked st, knit marked st; rep from * 3 more times, work to end.

Shape raglan

NEXT (DEC) ROW (RS): *Work in established patt to 2 sts before marked st, k2tog, p1, k2tog; rep from * 3 more times, work to end—8 sts dec'd.

Keeping the marked sts in reverse St st,

rep dec row every RS row 17 (18, 18, 19) more times—134 (142, 142, 150) sts.

Shape front neck

NEXT ROW (WS): BO 1, work the next 10 (11, 11, 12) sts and place on holder for front neck, work to end.

NEXT ROW (RS): BO 1, work the next 10 (11, 11, 12) sts and place on holder for front neck, work to end and dec for raglan as established—104 (110, 110, 116) sts. BO 3 sts at beg of next 10 rows and continue raglan shaping every RS row. *Note:* Neck shaping extends into the top of the sleeves; when not enough sts rem on each front to work raglan dec, work shaping on back and sleeves only, and when neck BO extends into top of sleeve, continue raglan shaping on back and back of sleeves only. Place rem sts on a holder.

Buttonband

Place the 9 sts from holder at left front on smaller needles and CO 1 (edge st) on side of band next to body—10 sts. Continue in rib, slipping first st of WS rows wyif and keeping edge st in garter st until band reaches beg of neck shaping when stretched slightly, ending with a RS row.

BO edge st and then work to end. Place rem 9 sts on a holder. Sew band to front edge. Mark placement for buttons, placing bottom marker opposite first buttonhole, then evenly space 4 more markers along buttonband so 6th buttonhole is worked in neckband.

Buttonhole band

Place the 9 sts from holder at right front on smaller needles and CO 1 (edge st) on side of band next to body—10 sts. Continue in rib, slipping first st of RS rows wyib and keeping edge st in garter st. *At the same time,* make 4 more buttonholes on RS rows to correspond to markers on buttonband. Continue as established until band reaches beg of neck shaping when stretched slightly, ending with a WS row. BO edge st, then work to end. Place rem 9 sts on a holder. Sew band to front edge.

Finishing

Weave in ends. Sew side and sleeve seams. Sew underarm seams.

Neckband

With smaller needles and RS facing, work 9 rib sts and k10 (11, 11, 12) sts from holders at right neck, pick up and k17 sts along right front edge and top of sleeve to holder, work sts from holder and dec evenly spaced over these sts to 31 (35, 35, 37) sts, pick up and k17 along left neck edge to holders, k10 (11, 11, 12) sts from holder, then work 9 sts from rem holder—105 (111, 111, 115) sts.

NEXT ROW (WS): Sl 1 wyif, *k1, p1; rep from * to end.

NEXT (BUTTONHOLE) ROW: Work 4 sts as established, BO 2 for rem buttonhole, work to end.

NEXT ROW: CO 2 sts over buttonhole gap.

Continue even in rib until neckband measures 1¼" (3 cm). BO all sts in ribbing.

Sew buttons to buttonband as marked.

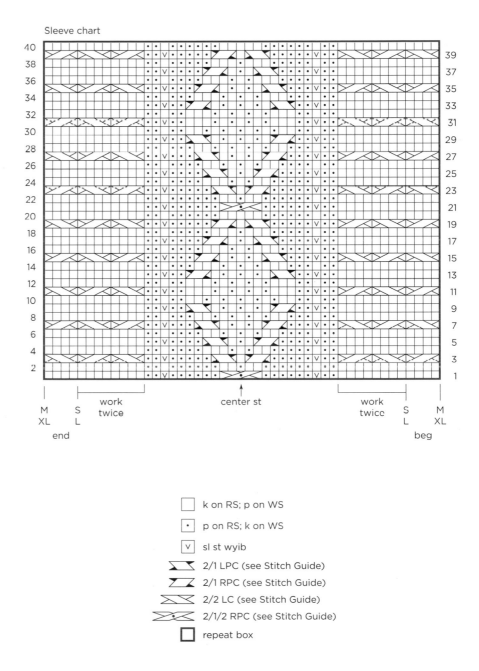

Sleeve chart

k on RS; p on WS
· p on RS; k on WS
v sl st wyib
2/1 LPC (see Stitch Guide)
2/1 RPC (see Stitch Guide)
2/2 LC (see Stitch Guide)
2/1/2 RPC (see Stitch Guide)
repeat box

Lace Patterns

At the most basic level, lace patterns are made with paired yarnovers and decreases. They are usually delicate and fine but some patterns can be worked with a chunky wool yarn and have a firmer look. In most lace patterns, every other row is a "resting" row where the stitches are worked as facing. However, on the most flowery and open lace motifs, yarnovers and decreases are made on every row.

Lana
Lace à la Cable

The vertical bands on the sweater's fronts and sleeves are actually lace patterns, but they look almost like cables because the decreases and yarnovers within the lace are not adjacent. It looks great on almost any figure and can be paired with pants, dresses, or skirts.

		S	M	L	XL
BUST	in	34½	38½	40½	44½
	cm	87.5	98	103	113
LENGTH	in	26½	26¾	27½	28
	cm	67.5	68	69	71

Yarn Chunky weight (Bulky #5). Shown in: Sandnes Garn Alfa (85% pure new wool, 15% mohair; 65 yd [60 m]/50 g): light gray #1042, 13 (14, 15, 16) balls.

Needles U.S. size 10 (6 mm). U.S. size 11 (7 mm). Adjust needle sizes if necessary to obtain the correct gauge.

Notions Stitch holders, tapestry needle, six 1" (25mm) leather buttons.

Gauge 13 sts and 19 rows = 4" (10 cm) in St st on larger needles.

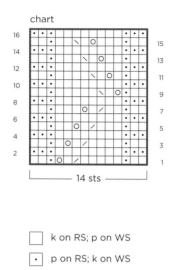

chart

16
14
12
10
8
6
4
2

15
13
11
9
7
5
3
1

|— 14 sts —|

  k on RS; p on WS

· p on RS; k on WS

o yo

∕ k2tog

∖ ssk

repeat box

Back

With smaller needles, CO 63 (69, 73, 79) sts. Work in garter st for 1¼" (3 cm), ending with a WS row.

NEXT (DEC) ROW (RS): K1 (edge st), k2tog, knit to last 3 sts, ssk, k1 (edge st)—2 sts dec'd. Work even until piece measures 2¼" (6 cm), ending with a WS row.

Change to larger needles.

Keeping edge sts in garter, continue in St st for 4 rows.

Rep dec row on next row, then every 12 rows 4 more times—51 (57, 61, 67) sts.

Work even until piece measures 14½ (14½, 15, 15)" (37 [37, 38, 38] cm), ending with a WS row.

NEXT (INC) ROW (RS): K1 (edge st), M1, knit to last st, M1, k1 (edge st)—2 sts inc'd.

Rep inc row every 8 rows twice more—57 (63, 67, 73) sts.

Work even until piece measures 18½ (18½, 19, 19)" (47 [47, 48, 48] cm), ending with a WS row.

Shape armhole

BO 2 (3, 3, 4) sts at beg of next 2 rows, 2 sts at beg of next 2 rows. Dec 1 st each end every RS row twice—45 (49, 53, 57) sts.

Work even until armhole measures 7 (7½, 7¾, 8¼)" (18 [19, 20, 21] cm), ending with a WS row.

Shape neck and shoulders

NEXT ROW (RS): BO 7 (7, 8, 9) sts, k7 (8, 9, 9), place center 17 (19, 19, 21) sts on holder for neck, join a second ball of yarn and knit to end.

NEXT ROW: BO 7 (7, 8, 9) sts, work to end—7 (8, 9, 9) sts rem each side.

BO 7 (8, 9, 9) sts at beg of next 2 rows.

Left Front

With smaller needles, CO 36 (39, 41, 44) sts. Work in garter st for 1¼" (3 cm), ending with a WS row.

NEXT (DEC) ROW (RS): K1 (edge st), k2tog, knit to last st, k1 (edge st)—1 st dec'd. Work even until piece measures 2¼" (6 cm), ending with a WS row.

Change to larger needles.

NEXT ROW (RS): K1 (edge st), k10 (12, 14, 16), work Row 1 of chart over next 14 sts, knit to end.

NEXT ROW: K6, p4 (5, 5, 6), work Row 2 of chart over next 14 sts, p10 (12, 14, 16), k1 (edge st).

Work 2 more rows as established.

Rep dec row on next row, then every 12 rows 4 more times—30 (33, 35, 38) sts.

Work even until piece measures 14½ (14½, 15, 15)" (37 [37, 38, 38] cm), ending with a WS row.

NEXT (INC) ROW (RS): K1 (edge st), M1, work to end—1 st inc'd.

Rep inc row every 8 rows twice more—33 (36, 38, 41) sts.

Work even until piece measures 18½ (18½, 19, 19)" (47 [47, 48, 48] cm), ending with a WS row.

Shape armhole

BO 2 (3, 3, 4) sts at beg of next row, 2 sts at beg of next RS row. Dec 1 st at beg of every RS row twice—27 (29, 31, 33) sts.

Work even until armhole measures 4¾ (5¼, 5¼, 5½)" (12 [13, 13, 14] cm), ending with a WS row.

Shape neck

SHORT-ROW 1 (RS): Work 22 (23, 25, 27) sts, turn.

SHORT-ROW 2 AND OTHER WS ROWS: Yo and work back to armhole edge.

SHORT-ROW 3: Work 19 (20, 22, 24) sts, turn.

SHORT-ROW 5: Work 17 (18, 20, 22) sts, turn.

SHORT-ROW 7: Work 15 (16, 18, 20) sts, turn.

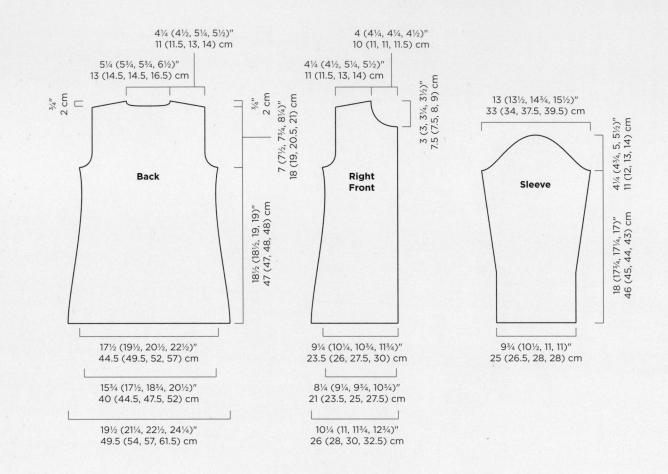

Back

4¼ (4½, 5¼, 5½)"
11 (11.5, 13, 14) cm

5¼ (5¾, 5¾, 6½)"
13 (14.5, 14.5, 16.5) cm

¾"
2 cm

¾"
2 cm

7 (7½, 7¾, 8¼)"
18 (19, 20.5, 21) cm

18½ (18½, 19, 19)"
47 (47, 48, 48) cm

17½ (19½, 20½, 22½)"
44.5 (49.5, 52, 57) cm

15¾ (17½, 18¾, 20½)"
40 (44.5, 47.5, 52) cm

19½ (21¼, 22½, 24¼)"
49.5 (54, 57, 61.5) cm

Right Front

4 (4¼, 4¼, 4½)"
10 (11, 11, 11.5) cm

4¼ (4½, 5¼, 5½)"
11 (11.5, 13, 14) cm

3 (3, 3¼, 3½)"
7.5 (7.5, 8, 9) cm

9¼ (10¼, 10¾, 11¾)"
23.5 (26, 27.5, 30) cm

8¼ (9¼, 9¾, 10¾)"
21 (23.5, 25, 27.5) cm

10¼ (11, 11¾, 12¾)"
26 (28, 30, 32.5) cm

Sleeve

13 (13½, 14¾, 15½)"
33 (34, 37.5, 39.5) cm

4¼ (4¾, 5, 5½)"
11 (12, 13, 14) cm

18 (17¾, 17¼, 17)"
46 (45, 44, 43) cm

9¾ (10½, 11, 11)"
25 (26.5, 28, 28) cm

SHORT-ROW 9: Work 14 (15, 17, 19) sts, turn.

Size XL only

SHORT-ROW 10: Yo and work back to armhole edge.

SHORT-ROW 11: Work 18 sts, turn.

All sizes

BO 7 sts at beg of next 2 (1, 0, 0) RS row(s), 8 sts at beg of next 0 (1, 1, 0)

RS row, then 9 sts at beg of next 0 (0, 1, 2) RS row(s). Place 13 (14, 14) neck sts and 4 (4, 4, 5) yo's on holder or scrap yarn.

Mark button placement along garter band, placing bottom button 7¾" (20 cm) from bottom edge, the top buttonhole will be worked in collar 1½" (4 cm) above the neckline, and evenly space the rem 4 buttons in between.

Right Front

With smaller needles, CO 36 (39, 41, 44) sts. Work in garter st for 1¼" (3 cm), ending with a WS row.

NEXT (DEC) ROW (RS): K1 (edge st), knit to last 3 sts, ssk, k1 (edge st)—1 st dec'd. Work even until piece measures 2¼" (6 cm), ending with a WS row.

Change to larger needles.

NEXT ROW (RS): K10 (11, 11, 12), work

Row 1 of chart over next 14 sts, knit to end.

NEXT ROW: K1 (edge st), p10 (12, 14, 16), work Row 2 of chart over next 14 sts, p4 (5, 5, 6), k6.

Work 2 more rows as established.

Rep dec row on next row, then every 12 rows 4 more times—30 (33, 35, 38) sts. *At the same time,* when piece measures 7¾" (20 cm), work buttonhole on next RS row as foll: k2, BO 2. On next row, CO 2 sts over gap. Make rem buttonholes as marked on left front. When shaping is complete, work even until piece measures 14½ (14½, 15, 15)" (37 [37, 38, 38] cm), ending with a WS row.

NEXT (INC) ROW (RS): Work to last st, M1, k1 (edge st)—1 st inc'd.

Rep inc row every 8 rows twice more—33 (36, 38, 41) sts.

Work even until piece measures 18½ (18½, 19, 19)" (47 [47, 48, 48] cm), ending with a RS row.

Shape armhole

BO 2 (3, 3, 4) sts at beg of next row, 2 sts at beg of next WS row. Dec 1 st at beg of every RS row twice—27 (29, 31, 33) sts.

Work even until armhole measures 4¾ (5¼, 5¼, 5½)" (12 [13, 13, 14] cm), ending with a RS row.

Shape neck

SHORT-ROW 1 (WS): Work 22 (23, 25, 27) sts, turn.

SHORT-ROWS 2, 4, 6, AND 8: Yo and work back to armhole edge.

SHORT-ROW 3: Work 19 (20, 22, 24) sts, turn.

SHORT-ROW 5: Work 17 (18, 20, 22) sts, turn.

SHORT-ROW 7: Work 15 (16, 18, 20) sts, turn.

SHORT-ROW 9: Work 14 (15, 17, 19) sts, turn.

Size XL only

SHORT-ROW 10: Yo and work back to armhole edge.

SHORT-ROW 11: Work 18 sts, turn.

All sizes

BO 7 sts at beg of next 2 (1, 0, 0) WS row(s), 8 sts at beg of next 0 (1, 1, 0) WS row, then 9 sts at beg of next 0 (0, 1, 2) WS row(s). Place 13 (14, 14) neck sts and 4 (4, 4, 5) yo's on holder or scrap yarn.

Sleeves

With smaller needles, CO 32 (34, 36, 36) sts. Work in garter st for 2¼" (6 cm), ending with a WS row.

Change to larger needles.

NEXT ROW (RS): K9 (10, 11, 11), work Row 1 of chart over next 14 sts, knit to end.

NEXT ROW: K1 (edge st), p8 (9, 10, 10), work Row 2 of chart over next 14 sts, p8 (9, 10, 10), k1 (edge st).

Continue in established patt until sleeve measures 6" (15 cm), ending with a WS row.

NEXT (INC) ROW (RS): K1 (edge st), M1, work to last st, M1, k1 (edge st)—2 sts inc'd.

Rep inc row every 14 (12, 10, 8) rows 4 (4, 5, 6) more times, work new sts in St st—42 (44, 48, 50) sts.

Work even until piece measures 18 (17¾, 17¼, 17)" (46 [45, 44, 43] cm), ending with a WS row.

Shape cap

BO 3 sts at beg of next 2 rows, 2 sts at beg of next 2 (2, 2, 4) rows. Dec 1 st each end every RS row 5 (6, 7, 7) times. BO 2 sts at beg of next 2 (2, 2, 4) rows, then 3 sts at beg of next 4 (4, 4, 2) rows—6 (6, 8, 8) sts. BO rem sts.

Finishing

Weave in ends. Block pieces to finished measurements.

Sew shoulder seams.

Neckband

Place neck sts and yos on smaller needles.

ROW 1 (RS): Knit sts from right front and knit each yo with next st, pick up and k13 (13, 14, 14) sts along right neck to back holder, k17 (19, 19, 21) sts from back neck, pick up and k13 (13, 14, 14) sts along left neck to front holder, knit sts from left front and knit each yo with next st—69 (73, 75, 79) sts.

Continue in garter st until collar measures 1½" (4 cm), ending with a WS row.

NEXT (BUTTONHOLE) ROW (RS): K2, BO 2 for buttonhole, knit to end.

NEXT ROW: CO 2 sts over gap.

Continue in garter st until collar measures 3¼" (8 cm). BO all sts knitwise.

Sew sleeve and side seams. Sew in sleeves. Sew buttons to left from where marked.

Cecilia
Romantic Circle Blouse

This lovely and flowery blouse was inspired by traditional lace knitting, not unlike lace doilies knit from the center out with complicated lace motifs. The increases in the circle consist of yarnovers that simultaneously shape the intricate pattern structure. This is a project for the most experienced knitters.

		S / M	L / XL
LENGTH	in	23½	25¾
	cm	59.5	65.5

Yarn Worsted weight (#4 Medium). Shown in: Permin Angel (70% kid mohair, 30% silk; 230 yd [210 m]/25 g): powder #04, 3 (3) balls.

Needles U.S. size 7 (4.5 mm): 24" (60 cm) and 32" (80 cm) circular (cir) for size S/M; U.S. size 8 (5 mm): 24" (60 cm) and 32" (80 cm) circular for size L/XL. Adjust needle size if necessary to obtain the correct gauge.

Notions Stitch markers (m), tapestry needle.

Gauge 19 sts and about 26 rows = 4" (10 cm) in St st on U.S. 7 (4.5 mm) needles for size S/M; 18 sts and about 25 rows = 4" (10 cm) in St st on U.S. 8 (5 mm) needles for size L/XL.

note:

The circle blouse is knit with the same stitch count for both sizes; only the needle size and, therefore, the gauge is different.

This blouse is worked from the top down, beginning with the shorter circular needle. Change to the longer circular needle when there are too many stitches to work comfortably on the shorter needle.

Stitch markers are used to mark the beginning of the round and the end of each repeat; slip markers as you come to them. Use a different color marker for the beginning of the round.

Blouse

With shorter cir needle for your size, CO 96 sts. Knit 3 rows and do not turn after last row. Join, being careful not to twist sts. Place marker (pm) for beg of rnd.

RNDS 1 AND 2: Knit.

RND 3: *Yo, k1 tbl, yo, k11, pm; rep from * to end of rnd—112 sts; 14 sts in each rep.

RND 4 AND ALL EVEN-NUMBERED RNDS: Knit all sts, except those knit through back loop (tbl) on previous rnd; always work those sts k1 tbl.

RND 5: *Yo, k3, yo, k11; rep from * to end of rnd—128 sts; 16 sts in each rep.

RND 7: *Yo, k5, yo, k4, sl 1, k2tog, psso, k4; rep from * to end of rnd.

RND 9: *Yo, k7, yo, k3, sl 1, k2tog, psso, k3; rep from * to end of rnd.

RND 11: *Yo, ssk, k5, k2tog, yo, k2, sl 1, k2tog, psso, k2; rep from * to end of rnd—112 sts; 14 sts in each rep.

RND 13: *Yo, k1 tbl, yo, ssk, k3, k2tog, yo, k1 tbl, yo, k1, sl 1, k2tog, psso, k1; rep from * to end of rnd.

RND 15: *Yo, k1 tbl, yo, k1, yo, k1 tbl, yo, ssk, k1, k2tog, yo, k1 tbl, yo, k1, yo, k1 tbl, yo, sl 1, k2tog, psso; rep from * to end of rnd—144 sts; 18 sts in each rep.

RND 17: *(K1 tbl, yo) 5 times, ssk, yo, sl 1, k2tog, psso, yo, k2tog, yo, (k1 tbl, yo) 6 times; rep from * to end of rnd—224 sts; 28 sts in each rep.

RND 19: *(Ssk, yo) 5 times, ssk, k1, (k2tog, yo) 6 times, k3, yo; rep from * to end of rnd.

RND 21: *(Ssk, yo) 5 times, sl 1, k2tog, psso, (yo, k2tog) 5 times, yo, k5, yo; rep from * to end of rnd.

RND 23: *(Yo, ssk) 5 times, k1, (k2tog, yo) 5 times, k7; rep from * to end of rnd.

RND 25: *Yo, k1 tbl, (yo, ssk) 4 times, yo, sl 1, k2tog, psso, (yo, k2tog) 4 times, yo, k1 tbl, yo, ssk, k3, k2tog; rep from * to end of rnd.

RND 27: *Yo, k3, (yo, ssk) 4 times, k1, (k2tog, yo) 4 times, k3, yo, ssk, k1, k2tog; rep from * to end of rnd.

RND 29: *Yo, k5, (yo, ssk) 3 times, yo, sl 1, k2tog, psso, (yo, k2tog) 3 times, yo, k5, yo, sl 1, k2tog, psso; rep from * to end of rnd.

RND 31: *Ssk, k5, (yo, ssk) 3 times, k1, (k2tog, yo) 3 times, k5, k2tog, yo, k1 tbl, yo; rep from * to end of rnd.

RND 33: *Sl 1, k2tog, psso, k4, (yo, ssk) twice, yo, sl 1, k2tog, psso, (yo, k2tog) twice, yo, k4, k3tog, yo, k3, yo; rep from * to end of rnd—208 sts; 26 sts in each rep.

RND 35: *Ssk, k4, (yo, ssk) twice, k1, (k2tog, yo) twice, k4, k2tog, yo, k1 tbl, yo, sl 1, k2tog, psso, yo, k1 tbl, yo; rep from * to end of rnd.

RND 37: *Ssk, k4, yo, ssk, yo, sl 1, k2tog, psso, yo, k2tog, yo, k4, k2tog, yo, k3, yo, k1 tbl, yo, k3, yo; rep from * to end of rnd—224 sts; 28 sts in each rep.

RND 39: *Ssk, k4, yo, ssk, k1 tbl, k2tog, yo, k4, k2tog, yo, k1 tbl, yo, sl 1, k2tog, psso, yo, k3, yo, sl 1, k2tog, psso, yo, k1 tbl, yo; rep from * to end of rnd.

RND 41: *Ssk, k4, yo, sl 1, k2tog, psso, yo, k4, k2tog, yo, k3, yo, k1 tbl, yo, ssk, k1, k2tog, yo, k1 tbl, yo, k3, yo; rep from * to end of rnd—240 sts; 30 sts in each rep.

RND 43: *Ssk, k9, k2tog, yo, k1 tbl, yo, sl 1, k2tog, psso, yo, (k3, yo, sl 1, k2tog, psso, yo) twice, k1 tbl. yo; rep from * to end of rnd.

RND 45: *Ssk, k7, k2tog, yo, k3, yo, k1 tbl, yo, (ssk, k1, k2tog, yo, k1 tbl, yo) twice, k3, yo; rep from * to end of rnd—256 sts; 32 sts in each rep.

RND 47: *Ssk, k5, k2tog, yo, k1 tbl, yo, sl 1, k2tog, psso, (yo, k3, yo, sl 1, k2tog, psso) 3 times, yo, k1 tbl, yo; rep from * to end of rnd.

RND 49: *Ssk, k3, k2tog, yo, k3, yo, k1 tbl, yo, (ssk, k1, k2tog, yo, k1 tbl, yo) 3 times, k3, yo; rep from * to end of rnd—272 sts; 34 sts in each rep.

RND 51: *Ssk, k1, k2tog, yo, k1 tbl, yo, sl 1, k2tog, psso, (yo, k3, yo, sl 1, k2tog, psso) 4 times, yo, k1 tbl, yo; rep from * to end of rnd.

RND 53: *Yo, sl 1, k2tog, psso, yo, k3, yo, k1 tbl, yo, (ssk, k1, k2tog, yo, k1 tbl, yo) 4 times, k3; rep from * to end of rnd—288 sts; 36 sts in each rnd.

RND 55: *(Yo, k3, yo, sl 1, k2tog, psso) 6 times; rep from * to end of rnd.

RND 57: *(Ssk, k1, k2tog, yo, k1 tbl, yo) 3 times, k5, yo, k1 tbl, yo, (ssk, k1, k2tog, yo, k1 tbl, yo) twice; rep from * to end of rnd—304 sts; 38 sts in each rnd.

RND 59: *(Sl 1, k2tog, psso, yo, k3, yo) twice, sl 1, k2tog, psso, yo, k11, yo, (sl 1, k2tog, psso, yo, k3, yo) twice; rep from * to end of rnd.

RND 61: *(Yo, k1 tbl, yo, ssk, k1, k2tog) twice, yo, k1 tbl, yo, k13, (yo, k1 tbl, yo, ssk, k1, k2tog) twice; rep from * to end of rnd—320 sts; 40 sts in each rep.

RND 63: *(Yo, k3, yo, sl 1, k2tog, psso) twice, yo, k19, yo, sl 1, k2tog, psso, yo, k3, yo, sl 1, k2tog, psso; rep from * to end of rnd.

RND 65: *(Ssk, k1, k2tog, yo, k1 tbl, yo)

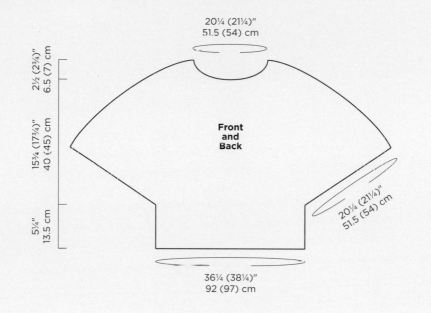

20¼ (21¼)"
51.5 (54) cm

2½ (2¾)"
6.5 (7) cm

15¾ (17¾)"
40 (45) cm

5¼"
13.5 cm

Front
and
Back

20¼ (21¼)"
51.5 (54) cm

36¼ (38¼)"
92 (97) cm

twice, k21, yo, k1 tbl, yo, ssk, k1, k2tog, yo, k1 tbl, yo; rep from * to end of rnd—336 sts; 42 sts in each rep.

RND 67: *Sl 1, k2tog, psso, yo, k3, yo, sl 1, k2tog, psso, yo, k27, yo, sl 1, k2tog, psso, yo, k3, yo; rep from to end of rnd.

RND 69: *Yo, k1 tbl, yo, ssk, k1, k2tog, yo, k1 tbl, yo, k29, yo, k1 tbl, yo, ssk, k1, k2tog; rep from * to end of rnd—352 sts; 44 sts in each rep.

RND 71: *Yo, k3, yo, sl 1, k2tog, psso, yo, k35, yo, sl 1, k2tog, psso; rep from * to end of rnd.

RND 73: *Ssk, k1, k2tog, yo, k1 tbl, yo, k37, yo, k1 tbl, yo; rep from * to end of rnd—368 sts; 46 sts in each rep.

RND 75: *Yo, sl 1, k2tog, psso, yo, k43; rep from * to end of rnd.

RND 77: Remove beg of rnd m, k1, replace beg of rnd m, *yo, k1 tbl, yo, k45; rep from * to end of rnd,

removing marker at end of each rep—384 sts; 48 sts in each rep.

Knit 21 rnds even.

Sleeve edgings

RND 99: Remove beg of rnd m, k1, replace beg of rnd m, k4, *(k2tog, yo, k1, yo, ssk, k7) 7 times, k2tog, yo, k1, yo, ssk,* k103; rep from * to * once more, k99.

RND 101: K3, *(k2tog, yo, k3, yo, ssk, k5) 7 times, k2tog, yo, k3, yo, ssk,* k101; rep from * to * once more, k98.

RND 103: K2, *(k2tog, yo, ssk, yo, k1, yo, k2tog, yo, ssk, k3) 7 times, k2tog, yo, ssk, yo, k1, yo, k2tog, yo, ssk,* k99; rep from * to * once more, k97.

RND 105: *(K1, k2tog, yo, k2, yo, sl 1, k2tog, psso, yo, k2, yo, ssk) 8 times, k96; rep from * once more.

RND 107: *K2tog, yo, (k3, k2tog, yo, k4, yo, sl 1, k2tog, psso, yo) 7 times,

k3, k2tog, yo, k4, yo, ssk, k95; rep from * once more.

RND 108: Knit.

RND 109: *P96, k96; rep from * once more.

RNDS 110 AND 111: Rep Rnds 108 and 109.

Divide body and sleeves

RND 112: *BO 96, (k1, p1) 4 times, (k2tog, [p1, k1] 3 times, p1) 9 times, k2tog, (p1, k1) twice, p1; rep from * once more—172 sts.

Continue in k1, p1 rib for 5¼" (13.5 cm). BO in ribbing.

Finishing

Weave in ends. Sew ends of neckband together. Block piece to measurements.

Coco
So Small and Fine

Here's an absolutely classic cardigan you can wear for many years. It will look good on almost anyone and can be fashioned for both fine and more casual wear. You'll memorize the lace pattern quickly because the same four rows are repeated throughout.

		S / M	M / L	XL
BUST	in	36	40¾	45¾
	cm	91.5	103.5	116
LENGTH	in	20¼	21	21¾
	cm	51.5	53.5	55

Yarn Fingering weight (Superfine #1). Shown in: Isager Highland (100% lambswool; 306 yd [280 m]/50 g): maize, 4 (5, 6) balls.

Needles U.S. size 4 (3.5 mm): straight, and 32" (80 cm) circular (cir). U.S. size 6 (4 mm): straight. Adjust needle sizes if necessary to obtain the correct gauge.

Notions Stitch markers (m), stitch holders, tapestry needle, six ⅝" (16 mm) mother-of-pearl buttons.

Gauge 23 sts and 32 rows = 4" (10 cm) in lace pattern on larger needles.

STITCH GUIDE

LACE PATTERN
(multiple of 7 sts + 2)

ROW 1 (RS): K1 (edge st), *k1, k2tog, yo, k1, yo, ssk, k1; rep from * to last st, k1 (edge st).

ROWS 2 AND 4: K1 (edge st), purl to last st, k1 (edge st).

ROW 3: K1 (edge st), *k2tog, yo, k3, yo, ssk; rep from * to last st, k1 (edge st).

Rep Rows 1–4 for patt.

SEED STITCH
(multiple of 2 sts)

ROW 1: *K, p1; rep from * across.

ROW 2: *P1, k1; rep from * across.

Rep Rows 1–2 for patt.

notes:

It is not always possible to work a complete stitch rep when increasing and decreasing at the beginning and end of a row. Each yarnover and decrease must always be worked as pairs in the pattern, so, if there are not enough stitches to work both the yarnover and decrease, simply work those sts in St st.

Since the knitting is very lofty, make sure that you don't sew the seams too tightly—it is easy to make them inelastic.

On our cardigan, the buttons have been sewn on with the back of the button facing.

POCKET LINING *(make 2)*

With larger needles, CO 22 (24, 25) sts. Work in St st for 3½" (9 cm), beg and end with a WS row. Place sts on a holder.

Back

With smaller needles, CO 100 (114, 128) sts. Work in seed st for 1" (2.5 cm), ending with a WS row.

Change to larger needles. Continue in Lace patt until piece measures 2" (5 cm), ending with a WS row.

NEXT (DEC) ROW (RS): K1 (edge st), k2tog, work in patter as established to last 3 sts, ssk, k1 (edge st)—2 sts dec'd.

Rep dec row every 18 rows twice more—94 (108, 122) sts.

Work even until piece measures 9 (9½, 9¾)" (23 [24, 25] cm), ending with a WS row.

NEXT (INC) ROW (RS): K1, M1, work in established patt to last st, M1, k1—2 sts inc'd.

Rep inc row every 8 rows twice more—100 (114, 128) sts.

Work even until piece measures 13¼" (34.5 cm), ending with a WS row.

Shape armholes

BO 5 sts at beg of next 0 (2, 2) rows, 3 sts at beg of next 2 rows, 2 sts at beg of next 4 rows. Dec 1 st each end every RS row 3 (2, 2) times—80 (86, 100) sts. Work even until armhole measures 6¼ (6¾, 7)" (16 [17, 18] cm), ending with a WS row.

Shape neck and shoulders

NEXT ROW (RS): BO 6 (7, 9) sts, work 14 (16, 20) sts in established patt, place center 40 (40, 42) sts on a holder for neck, join a second ball of yarn and work to end. Work each side separately.

NEXT ROW: BO 6 (7, 9) sts, work to end—14 (16, 20) sts rem each side.

BO 7 (8, 10) sts at beg of next 4 rows.

Left Front

With smaller needles, CO 50 (57, 64) sts. Work in seed st for 1" (2.5 cm), ending with a WS row and inc 1 st on last row—51 (58, 65) sts.

Change to larger needles. Continue in Lace patt until piece measures 2" (5 cm), ending with a WS row. Place marker (pm) 12 (14, 18) sts from front edge and 16 (19, 21) sts from side edge; 22 (24, 25) sts are between markers for pocket.

NEXT (DEC) ROW (RS): K1 (edge st), k2tog, work in established patt to last st, k1 (edge st)—1 st dec'd.

Rep dec row every 18 rows twice more—48 (55, 62) sts. *At the same time,* when piece measures 4½" (11.5 cm), end with a WS row. Place sts for one pocket on needle to beg with a RS row.

NEXT ROW (RS): Work in established patt to first m, place next 22 sts on holder for pocket, work 22 pocket lining sts in Lace patt, then work rem front sts.

Work even until piece measures 9 (9½, 9¾)" (23 [24, 25] cm), ending with a WS row.

NEXT (INC) ROW (RS):: K1, M1, work in established patt to last st, k1—1 st inc'd.

Rep inc row every 8 rows twice more—51 (58, 65) sts.

Work even until piece measures 13¼" (34.5 cm), ending with a WS row.

Shape armhole and neck

BO 5 sts at beg of next 0 (1, 1) RS row, 3 sts at beg of next RS row, 2 sts at beg of next 2 RS rows. Dec 1 st at beg of every RS row 3 (2, 2) times. *At the same time,* dec 1 st at neck edge every RS row 15 (13, 13) times, then every 4 rows 6 (8, 9) times as foll: work as established to last 3 sts, ssk, k1 (edge st).

At the same time, when armhole measures 6¼ (6¾, 7)" (16 [17, 18] cm), end with a WS row.

Shape shoulder

BO 6 (7, 9) sts at beg of next RS row, then 7 (8, 10) sts at beg of next 2 RS rows.

Right Front

With smaller needles, CO 50 (57, 64) sts. Work in seed st for 1" (2.5 cm), ending with a WS row and inc 1 st on last row—51 (58, 65) sts.

Change to larger needles. Continue in Lace patt until piece measures 2" (5 cm), ending with a WS row. Place marker (pm) 12 (14, 18) sts from front edge and 16 (19, 21) sts from side edge; 22 (24, 25) sts are between markers for pocket.

NEXT (DEC) ROW (RS): K1 (edge st), work in established patt to last 3 sts, ssk, k1 (edge st)—1 st dec'd.

Lace chart

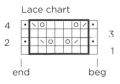

k on RS; p on WS

p on RS; k on WS

yo

k2tog

ssk

repeat box

Rep dec row every 18 rows twice more—48 (55, 62) sts. *At the same time,* when piece measures 4½" (11.5 cm), end with a WS row. Place sts for one pocket on needle to beg with a RS row.

NEXT ROW (RS): Work in established patt to first m, place next 22 sts on holder for pocket, work 22 pocket lining sts in Lace patt, then work rem front sts.

Work even until piece measures 9 (9½, 9¾)" (23 [24, 25] cm), ending with a WS row.

NEXT (INC) ROW (RS): K1 (edge st), work in established patt to last st, M1, k1—1 st inc'd.

Rep inc row every 8 rows twice more—51 (58, 65) sts.

Work even until piece measures 13¼" (34.5 cm), ending with a RS row.

Shape armhole and neck

BO 5 sts at beg of next 0 (1, 1) WS row, 3 sts at beg of next WS row, 2 sts at beg of next 2 WS rows. Dec 1 st at end of every RS row 3 (2, 2) times. *At the same time,* dec 1 st at neck edge every RS row 15 (13, 13) times, then every 4 rows 6 (8, 9) times as foll: k1 (edge st), k2tog, work as established to end.

At the same time, when armhole measures 6¼ (6¾, 7)" (16 [17, 18] cm), end with a RS row.

Shape shoulder

BO 6 (7, 9) sts at beg of next WS row, then 7 (8, 10) sts at beg of next 2 WS rows.

Sleeves

With smaller needles, CO 58 (58, 65) sts. Work in seed st for 1" (2.5 cm).

Change to larger needles. Work 8 rows in Lace patt.

NEXT (INC) ROW (RS): K1 (edge st), M1, work in established patt to last st, M1, k1 (edge st)—2 sts inc'd.

Rep inc row every 10 (8, 8) rows 10 (13, 13) times more—80 (86, 93) sts. Work new sts into pattern when yarnover and dec can be worked together. Work even until piece measures 16½ (16¾, 17)" (42 [42.5, 43] cm), ending with a WS row.

Shape cap

BO 5 sts at beg of next 0 (2, 2) rows, 3 sts at beg of next 2 rows, 2 sts at beg of next 4 (2, 2) rows. Dec 1 st each end every 4 rows 3 times. BO 2 sts at beg of next 8 (10, 10) rows, then BO 3 sts at beg of next 6 rows—26 (22, 29) sts. BO rem sts.

Finishing

Weave in ends. Block pieces to finished measurements.

Sew edges of pocket linings to WS.

Pocket edge

Place 22 (24, 25) sts for one pocket on smaller needle. Work in seed st for 1" (2.5 cm). BO all sts in patt. Sew ends of seed st band to RS.

Work pocket edge on rem pocket same as first.

Sew shoulder seams.

Buttonband

With cir needle and RS facing, beg at bottom of right front edge, pick up and k81 sts along right front to beg of neck shaping, 45 (47, 51) sts along right neck to holder, k40 (40, 42) sts from holder, pick up and k45 (47, 51) sts along left neck to beg of neck shaping, then 81 sts along left front to bottom edge—292 (296, 306) sts.

Work 3 rows in seed st.

NEXT (BUTTONHOLE) ROW (RS): Work 3 sts in established patt, *BO 2 for buttonhole, work 13 sts; rep from * 4 times more, BO 2 for buttonhole, work to end.

NEXT ROW: CO 2 sts over each buttonhole gap.

Work even until band measures 1" (2.5 cm). BO all sts in patt.

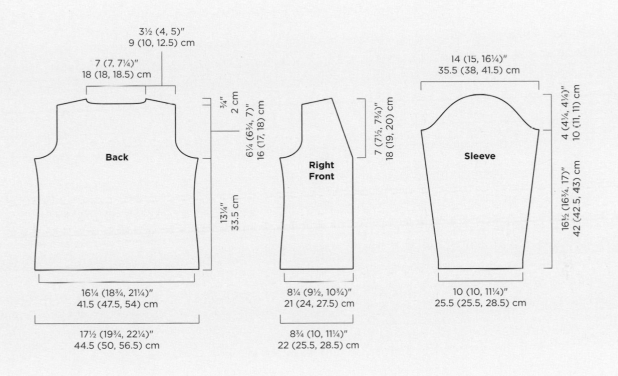

3½ (4, 5)"
9 (10, 12.5) cm

7 (7, 7¼)"
18 (18, 18.5) cm

¾"
2 cm

6¼ (6¾, 7)"
16 (17, 18) cm

13¼"
33.5 cm

Back

7 (7½, 7¾)"
18 (19, 20) cm

Right Front

8¼ (9½, 10¾)"
21 (24, 27.5) cm

8¾ (10, 11¼)"
22 (25.5, 28.5) cm

16¼ (18¾, 21¼)"
41.5 (47.5, 54) cm

17½ (19¾, 22¼)"
44.5 (50, 56.5) cm

14 (15, 16¼)"
35.5 (38, 41.5) cm

4 (4¼, 4¼)"
10 (11, 11) cm

16½ (16¾, 17)"
42 (42.5, 43) cm

Sleeve

10 (10, 11¼)"
25.5 (25.5, 28.5) cm

Vicky
Reversible Vest in Net Pattern

Here's a vest anyone can knit. This casual vest is made with two adjoined strips knit in an easy net lace pattern. The strips are sewn together at three places—totally easy—a concept that can be adapted for other patterns and yarns.

		One Size
LENGTH AT CENTER BACK	in	26
	cm	66

Yarn Fingering weight (Superfine #1). Shown in: Sandnes Garn Silk Mohair (60% kid mohair, 25% silk, 15% wool; 306 yd [280 m]/50 g): gray #1076, 2 balls.

Needles U.S. size 10 (6 mm): straight. Adjust needle size if necessary to obtain the correct gauge.

Notions Tapestry needle.

Gauge 15 sts and 20 rows = 4" (10 cm) in lace pattern.

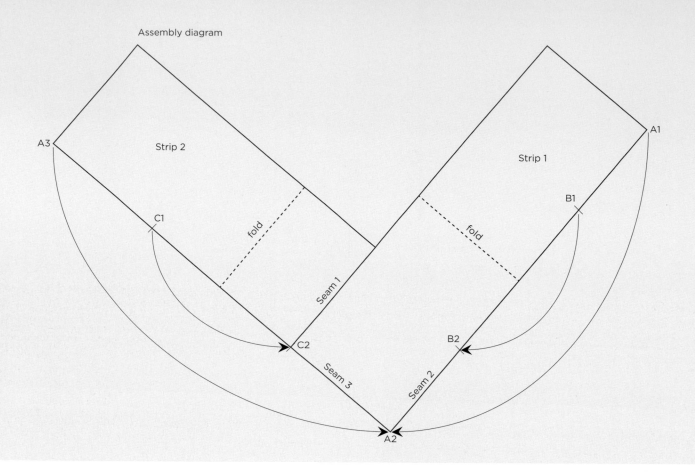

Assembly diagram

Strip 1

CO 62 sts loosely.

ROW 1 (RS): K1 (edge st), *p2tog, yo, p2; rep from * to last st, k1 (edge st).

ROW 2: K1 (edge st), *ssk, yo, k2; rep from * to last st, k1 (edge st).

Rep Rows 1–2 until piece measures about 47" (119.5 cm) long and 15½" (39.5 cm) wide when stretched slightly. BO all sts loosely.

Strip 2

Make same as Strip A until piece measures about 37½" (95 cm) long. BO all sts loosely.

Finishing

Weave in ends. Block pieces to finished measurements.

Assembly

With RS facing, sew strips together as shown in assembly diagram. Sew narrow seams as neatly as possible so that the vest is completely reversible.

SEAM 1: Sew one short end of Strip 2 to lower end of one long side of Strip 1.

SEAM 2: Fold Strip 1 with WS together. Sew the sides together from A to B [about 12½" (32 cm)], leaving about 11" (28 cm) open for armhole.

SEAM 3: Fold Stripe 2 with WS together, and points A3 and C1 meet points A2 and C2. Sew edges together between A and C, leaving about 11" (28 cm) open for armhole.

Holly
Lace Neck Warmer

You can easily wear a neck warmer instead of a scarf but don't keep it hidden under your coat. The edging on this neck warmer is so lovely it begs to be seen.

TOP CIRCUMFERENCE	in	19
	cm	48.5
LENGTH	in	9
	cm	23

Yarn Worsted weight (Medium #4). Shown in: Grignasco Loden (50% lambswool, 25% alpaca, 25% viscose; 120 yd [110 m]/50 g): blue #593, 1 ball.

Needles U.S. size 7 (4.5 mm): 16" (40 cm) circular (cir). Adjust needle size if necessary to obtain the correct gauge.

Notions Stitch marker, tapestry needle.

Gauge 19 sts and 24 rows = 4" (10 cm) in lace pattern.

note:

On chart Rnds 13, 15, and 47, slip the last stitch of the previous round back to the left-hand needle and use that to work the first decrease so the pattern remains properly aligned.

Neck Warmer

CO 110 sts loosely. Join, being careful not to twist sts. Place marker (pm) for beg of rnd.

RND 1: Beg at arrow on right-hand side of chart and work 12 sts, work 22 st rep 4 times, work rem 10 sts of chart.

Continue as established to end of chart—90 sts.

Knit 5 rnds. BO all sts loosely (the edge will roll to the outside).

Weave in ends.

chart

work 4 times

end

beg

	k on RS; p on WS
·	p on RS; k on WS
ℓ	k1 tbl
o	yo
∕	k2tog
∖	ssk
∧	s2pk (see Stitch Guide)
	no stitch
	do not work this st; it is used as the first st of the dec worked at the beg of next rnd
	repeat box

Yarns

The yarns listed below are those used for the designs in this book. The gauge (number of sts in 4" [10 cm]) is that given in the book. If no gauge is listed, it means that the yarn was worked together with another yarn and not alone.

Alfa from Sandnes Garn: 85% pure new wool, 15% mohair, 50 g = 65.6 yards (60 meters), 13 sts in St st on U.S. size 11 (7 mm) needles.

Angel from Permin: 70% kid mohair, 30% silk, 25 g = 229.5 yards (210 meters), 19–18 sts on U.S. size 7–8 (4.5–5 mm) needles.

Alpaca 1 from Isager: 100% alpaca, 100 g = 875 yards (800 meters).

Alpaca 2 from Isager: 50% alpaca, 50% Merino lamb's wool, 100 g = 547 yards (500 meters), 27 sts in St st on U.S. size 2.5 (3 mm) needles.

Alpaca Silk from Hjertegarn: 60% alpaca, 30% Merino wool, 10% silk, 50 g = 180 yards (165 meters), 26 sts in St st on U.S. size 2.5 (3 mm) needles.

Alpaca from Sandnes Garn: 100% baby alpaca, 50 g = 120 yards (110 meters), 22 sts in St st on U.S. size 4 (3.5) needles.

Camel+Merino from Onion: 70% Merino wool, 30% camel, 50 g = 120 yards (110 meters), 17 sts in garter st on U.S. size 8 (5 mm) needles.

Felted Tweed Aran from Rowan/Coats HP: 50% Merino wool, 25% alpaca, 25% viscose, 50 g = 95 yards (87 meters), 15 sts in St st on U.S. size 9 (5.5 mm) needles.

Felted Tweed DK from Rowan/Coats HP: 50% Merino wool, 25% alpaca, 25% viscose, 50 g = 191 yards (175 meters), 22 sts in St st on U.S. size 6 (4 mm) needles.

Fritidsgarn from Sandnes Garn: 100% pure new wool, 50 g = 76.5 yards (70 meters), 14 sts in St st on U.S. size 10 (6 mm) needles.

Highland from Isager: 100% lamb's wool, 50 g = 306 yards (280 meters), 23 sts in lace pattern on U.S. size 6 (4 mm) needles.

Kidmohair from BC Garn: 70% kidmohair, 30% polyamid, 25 g = 246 yards (225 meters).

Loden from Grignasco/Gepard Yarn: 50% lamb's wool, 25% viscose, 25% alpaca, 50 g = 120 yards (110 meters), 18 sts in St st on U.S. size 8 (5 mm) needles.

Puno from Gepard: 68% baby alpaca, 22% mixed synthetic fiber (netting), 10% Merino wool, 50 g = 120 yards (110 meters), 12 sts in St st on U.S. size 11 (8 mm) needles.

Semilla from BC Garn: 100% ecological wool, dyed with environmentally safe dye matter, 50 g = 175 yards (160 meters), 22 sts on U.S. size 6 (4 mm) needles.

Silkbloom Fino from BC Garn: 55% Merino wool, 45% silk, 50 g = 219 yards (200 meters), 25 sts in St st on U.S. size 4 (3.5 mm) needles.

Silk Mohair from Sandnes Garn: 60% kid mohair, 25% silk, 15% wool, 50 g = 306 yards (280 meters), 15 sts in lace pattern on U.S. size 10 (6 mm) needles.

Sisu from Sandnes Garn: 80% wool, 20% nylon, 50 g = 175 yards (160 meters), 27 sts in St st on U.S. size 2.5 (3 mm) needles.

Spinni from Isager: 100% wool, single ply, 100 g = 667 yards (610 meters).

Tweed from Wilfert's: 80% wool, 20% polyamid, 50 g = 115 yards (105 meters), 17 sts in St st on U.S. size 9 (5.5 mm) needles.

Sources for Yarns

In the USA

ISAGER
TUTTO Opal-Isager
218 Galisteo St.
Santa Fe, NM 87501
(505) 982-8356
www.knitisager.com

PERMIN
Distributed by Wichelt Imports Inc.

N162 Hwy. 35
Stoddard, WI 54658
www.wichelt.com

ROWAN YARNS
Distributed by
Westminster Fibers Inc.

165 Ledge St.
Nashua, NH 03060
(800) 445-9276
www.westminsterfibers.com

SANDNES GARN
Distributed by Swedish Yarn Import

PO Box 2609
126-A Wade St.
Jamestown, NC 27282
www.swedishyarn.com

Outside the USA

BC GARN
Albuen 56 A
6000 Kolding
Denmark
www.bcgarn.dk

GEPARD OG GRIGNASCO
Gl Jernbanevej 7-2800
Lyngby
Denmark
www.gepardgarn.dk

HJERTEGARN
Fallesgårdevej 8A, Grønhøj
7470 Karup
Denmark
www.hjertegarn.dk

ONION
Bøssebjerg 3
4500 Nykøbing Sj
Denmark
www.onion.dk

WILFERT'S
www.wilferts.dk

Index

abbreviations 8

Blocks for a Sweater 54–59

charts 7
Classic Cable Sweater 118–123

Detail Features on Both Front and
    Back sweater 38–44

edge stitches 7

Feminine Guernsey sweater, A 66–71
Feminine Hoodie 72–77
finishing 8
Flattering Vintage-Style shrug 22–25

Garter Stitch Coat with Tucks 16–21
Garter Stitch Sweater with Raglan
    Shaping 12–15
gauge 7

instructions, reading 7

Lace à la Cable sweater 126–131
Lace Neck Warmer 146–148
Little Cabled Vest 112–117
Long Garter Stitch Sweater 30–35

More Ways than One hats 50–53
Moss Stitch Jacket 88–93

One Sweater, Two Lengths 100–107

Reversible Poncho 84–87
Reversible Vest in Net Pattern
    142–145
Romantic Circle Blouse 132–135

Scarf with Lace Edging 26–29
Seed Stitch Wrist Warmers 108–111
setting stitches aside 7
Short-sleeve Vest with Leaf Motifs
    60–63
sizes chart 6
sizes, adjusting 6
So Small and Fine sweater 136–141
Softest Leaf sweater, The 44–49
stitches, edge 7; setting aside 7
Sweet and Nostalgic sweater 78–83
symbol key 9

Top with Cap Sleeves 96–99

yarn 7

Love timeless knitwear
that offers fashionable and feminine style?

Explore these beautiful titles from Interweave

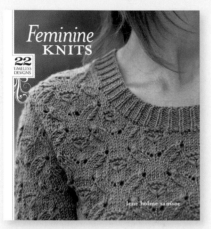

Feminine Knits
22 Timeless Designs

Lene Holme Samsøe

ISBN 978-1-59668-140-8
$22.95

French Girl Knits
*Innovative Techniques, Romantic
Details, and Feminine Designs*

Kristeen Griffin-Grimes

ISBN 978-1-59668-069-2
$24.95

Vintage Modern Knits
*Contemporary Designs using
Classic Techniques*

Courtney Kelley and
Kate Gagnon Osborn

ISBN 978-1-59668-240-5
$24.95

INTERWEAVE
KNITS

From cover to cover, *Interweave Knits* magazine
presents great projects for the beginner to the
advanced knitter. Every issue is packed full of
captivating smart designs, step-by-step instructions,
easy-to-understand illustrations, plus well-written,
lively articles sure to inspire. **Interweaveknits.com**

Join Knittingdaily.com, an online community
that shares your passion for knitting. You'll get
a free e-newsletter, free patterns, projects store,
a daily blog, event updates, galleries, tips and
techniques, and more. Sign up for *Knitting Daily* at
Knittingdaily.com

shop.knittingdaily.com